Captain Harry

Sea Fever

Written and Illustrated by

HARRY FURNISS

Printed in Victoria, Canada

National Library of Canada Cataloguing in Publication Data

Furniss, Harry, 1920-
  Memoirs two : sea fever
  ISBN 1-55212-820-2
  1. Furniss, Harry, 1920- 2. Pacific Coast (B.C.)--Biography.
3. Boats and boating--British Columbia--Pacific Coast. I. Title.
FC3845.P2Z49 2001a   971.1'104'092   C2001-911124-X
F1089.P2F87 2001

TRAFFORD

This book was published *on-demand* in cooperation with Trafford Publishing.
On-demand publishing is a unique process and service of making a book available for retail
sale to the public taking advantage of on-demand manufacturing and Internet marketing.
On-demand publishing includes promotions, retail sales, manufacturing, order fulfilment,
accounting and collecting royalties on behalf of the author.

Suite 6E, 2333 Government St., Victoria, B.C. V8T 4P4, CANADA
Phone   250-383-6864   Toll-free   1-888-232-4444 (Canada & US)
Fax   250-383-6804   E-mail   sales@trafford.com
Web site   www.trafford.com TRAFFORD PUBLISHING IS A DIVISION OF TRAFFORD HOLDINGS LTD.
Trafford Catalogue #01-0220   www.trafford.com/robots/01-0220.html

10   9   8   7   6   5   4   3

This is the second volume of Memoirs dealing with my life and times. It's about boats and the sea, a passionate hobby for most of my life, and covers experiences as both an amateur and professional sailor.

Yachting, as we called recreational boating in earlier years, proved a soothing change of pace after my hectic years of flying with the RCAF throughout World War Two. Those days were the subject of my first volume of Memoirs, titled "The Flying Game" ISBN 1-55212-513-0.

In preparing these salty tales, I have drawn liberally on my work as a staff writer, editor and columnist for the Vancouver Province newspaper, and similar work free-lancing, and as editor of the now-sadly defunct Northwest Sportsman, owned for many years by my great friend and treasured fishing companion, the late Jim Railton.

Sea Fever
MEMOIRS : TWO

Sea Dreams

It came as quite a surprise the other day to realize what a remarkable portion of my 80 plus years on this earth have been spent at sea.

Weekends, holidays, sabbaticals, occasional business trips and personal leisure time now total more than 7 years afloat. Put another way, that spells about 85 months, or 369 weeks, or 2591 days on the briny. Expressed as mileage, I have completed the equivalent of two round-the-world cruises.

While I have enjoyed six crossings of the Atlantic in regular steamships, the great majority of my time at sea has been in the small pleasure boats which I have owned over some 45 years. In the largest of these (with a temporary Masters Certificate) I carried out two seven-month charters up the BC coast for the federal Department of Fisheries. And in a smaller boat I re-visited many of those coastal havens during three six-month holidays after I retired.

The years have also included diverse interludes aboard yachts big and small belonging to friends, and one memorable period as First Officer aboard lumber baron H.R. MacMillan's 130-foot converted mine sweeper.

I sold my last yacht with considerable anguish (boat talk for facing more shipyard bills than I could handle) when I turned 71. I took up flying again and have found great solace in regularly visiting the old marine havens that I loved so long.

Beware the eye in the sky, my old friends — it could be Captain Harry .

⚓   ⚓   ⚓

The lure of the sea, they call it. That mysterious life-force which irresistibly draws us back to the ocean from whence we once crawled formless and insensitive, covered with slime and scales. That tang of saltwater and seaweed which like a powerful virus instantly re-programs the human brain box. Irrevocably.

Once smitten we spend the rest of our lives wallowing in a mystique shot through with phony glamour, surrounded by myths and backed by a thousand years of dubious folklore. There is no salvation this side of a snug berth in Davy Jones' locker.

Consider some of the crummy sentiment that has grown up about the sea — iron men and wooden ships and all that rot. For centuries children have been lulled to sleep by old crones chanting . . . "men that go down to the sea in ships . . . "

Whoever heard of going down to the sea in ships? You go down to the sea by foot, bicycle, horse or car and THEN you go to sea in ships. Elementary, eh?

Some people fancy an ancestral link. "Poor Furniss," they sigh, "can't help himself. Comes from a long line of seafarin' men, y'know. In his blood."

Nonsense. I come from a long line of city-farin' men whose only contact with water was the Saturday night bath. Never saw the sea (although I've see-sawed) until I moved to Vancouver. And didn't think much about it then until the incurable fever struck shortly after a departing West Vancouver neighbor (Fred Goodchild, editorial writer on The Province) bequeathed me his lifetime hoard of treasured Yachting and Rudder magazines.

Even a brief sampling of such concentrated reading is enough to galvanize frenzied activity. You start out dazed and dreamy-eyed and after a winter's toil in the garden shed emerge with a box-like scow which you launch with tremendous pride.

And the feeling that finally YOU HAVE ARRIVED in yachting circles !

Phooey. She's an ill-made, leaky punt of poor design, and you know it. And then, while you're paying off the lumber yard and putt-putting around the bay , the rest of the water world is thundering past in chrome-plated overnighters. Envy clutters your mental radar and quickly you are stuck on a psychological sandbar. Incoherence takes over and you jump up and down screaming salty curses that rhyme with NANTUCKET.

And as you loose complete control of your sanity and purse strings, you start firing off insane memos to innocent suppliers:

Purser:

Check this catalogue . . .
Are you sure we have adequate supplies aboard?
                                    Capt. Harry

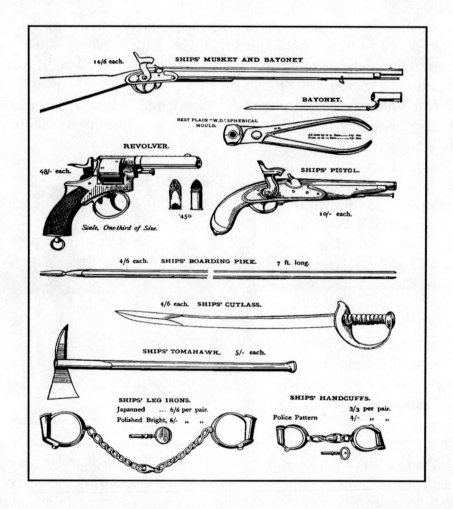

Dissatisfaction spreads like dry rot . You don't realize it at the time but you are suffering an acute attack of "tired oarlocks " which can only be cured by moving up the scale to a larger craft, with a bigger engine, with more accommodation, and well, y'know . . . a bit more class.

The little woman is little help. She-wants-that-great-big-one-over-there-and-if-money-doesn't-grow-on-trees-then-why-does-everyone-else-have-one-except-us?

The bank manager contributes to this madness. He can see a lifetime of interest payments rolling in and can't dish out the money fast enough. It's like drinking too much rum — you know you're going to have hell of a hangover when you wake up, BUT BY GOD IT FEELS GOOD RIGHT NOW !

Besides being in hock up to your eyeballs, the boss is raising hell because you're spending more time dreaming about your boat than his lousy widgets. His parting shot as you shove off on your first weekend, the icebox filled with steak and beer, rings ominously in your ears: "Have fun Harry. Don't hurry back. Lots of people here ready to take your job over."

You pop the hook down in a sheltered bay, scorch the steaks, knock off all the beer in a single orgy and crawl into the sack, too doped to think about tomorrow. Four hours later you awake with a jolt. The bay is lashed to a frenzy by a surprise southwester. Your new boat is dancing around like a bubble of water on a hot griddle. BY GOD SHE'S TINY !

Struggling into your new wet-weather clothes, you go on deck to try and figure out just how in hell to escape certain doom. Your new 12-battery spotlight shorts out, water cascades through a split in that new parka, your yachting cap blows away, the little woman is sniffling and the dog is sick all over your feet.

At the worst possible moment, the new $100 anchor line parts with a cheap twang, the waves slop into the non-self-bailing cockpit as the bucket rolls beam-on to the seas, the dinghy drifts off into the blackness and BY GOD WE'RE HEADED FOR THE ROCKS this time for sure.

Miraculously you stave off disaster, although you end up in bed with a frightful dose of pneumonia and the best set of shakes this side of the Sanatorium, a bill for damages from the dog (via the SPCA) and a divorce petition from the (ha!) better half.

Your job is gone. Your money, your luck. Your wife will take the house, if you throw in the car and a couple of thousand a month. Which finally leaves you all alone with your boat in a blissful world of solitude.

Your awkward home-built scow, having survived the fierce elements in the unforgiving crucible of the sea, now assumes a new role in your life. You may no longer be Captain of your Fate, but you're sure as hell Captain of this Yacht.

WHAT PRICE THE LURE OF THE SEA?

A Pod of Putzys

In the early summer of 1955, after two months of superhuman moonlighting in a shed behind Sangster's Boatworks on West Georgia Street, PUTZY was finally ready for launching.

I wanted to call her HUNTZY after our helpful Bank of Montreal manager in West Vancouver. However, the First Mate — my ever-loving wife Enid — campaigned vigorously for continuation of the PUTZY name which had so far graced three Furniss-built creations — a sailing paddleboard, an 8-foot sailing Sabot dinghy, and the 16-foot inboard day fisherman.

The name PUTZY proved to be an eye-catcher. After it appeared on the transom of the 16-footer, and in newspaper stories I wrote about building her in the basement, we met Europeans who smiled knowingly and told us **(vink, vink, knod, knod)** that it meant "little sweetheart."

Other Europeans, with equal assertiveness, said flatly that it meant something else, quite vulgar.

Actually, the name was inspired by the staccato blatt of the stout-hearted Briggs and Stratton one-lungers which putt-putted small rental boats so reliably around local fishing grounds in those days.

Wrap a cord around the flywheel, tug, and presto — 8.5 horsepower and an inboard muffler hot enough to toast marshmallows on

As time passed and I wrote more and more about the care and feeding of PUTZYs, our names became linked and the local notoriety was enjoyable.

So we christened the new craft PUTZY TOO in a spirited if not original mood before a thirsting crowd of friends.

My new dreamboat had been rolled out of a shed called "the green-house" on a cradle and trundled to a crane at the end of the Sangster wharf.

Following my fishing pal Pintail's instructions to the letter, I carefully uncorked the champagne, wet a finger (lightly) and dabbed PUTZY TOO's bow.

He's right, you know: much more fun sipping the bubbly from goblets than soaking the wharf with murky puddles of froth.

As the crane set PUTZY TOO gently afloat on the oily waters of Van-couver Harbor I noted with considerable satisfaction that she floated ex-actly on her boot top which I had painted freehand. That damn "greenhouse" was so narrow I couldn't get my nose more than two inches away from the hull.

The shed was called the greenhouse because of the translucent panels let into the roof as skylights when the building served as the Sangster paint shop. Bob had kindly let me use it rent free, so I shouldn't complain. Insult enough was my new long-shafted 25 hp Johnson (green) outboard on PUTZY's transom for Bob was an Evinrude (blue) dealer of many years standing.

Johnny (the motor) started easily and loaded to the gunnels with en-thusiastic guests I cruised slowly over to the Immigration Wharf where we raised Captain Murchison of the city fireboat. In deference to Murch's deepwater background, we let him pump a priming bucket of saltwater through our new marine toilet. Just in time, too, for the warmth of the day had drastically increased the consumption of beer and guests were danc-ing around, eager to inspect this piece of equipment.

The party ended predictably as the last drop of liquid refreshment gur-gled down the hatch. When all the guests had left I was finally able to re-alize the ultimate thrill of yacht ownership . . . pack up the empty bottles, wash the glasses, sweep up the *canapé* droppings, clean up the galley and toilet and pay off the wharf attendant.

However, as I worked I consoled myself that I was under the approv-ing gaze of fellow yachtsman D.K.Ludwig of New York, anchored close by in his 257-foot DAGNIN of Liberia. His eyes, as he leaned over his pol-ished teak deck-rail surrounded by white-jacketed stewards and dinner-jacketed guests, were positively green with envy for my simple life.

Daniel Ludwig was a naturalized American shipping tycoon, reputed to be one of the world's richest men. Yet, when he died in 1992, he left a paltry estate of US$ 1.2 billion.

His fabulous yacht (more opulent than Onassis' converted Royal Canadian Navy frigate) no doubt soaked up many millions in operating costs, but the bulk of Ludwig's huge fortune was lost in Brazil trying to turn those vast forests into the world's largest pulp and paper "factory."

The next morning the First Mate and I were aboard early and set course for our permanent berth at the West Vancouver Yacht Club at Fisherman's Cove. The bright, sunny day with deep blue skies and azure sea contrasted majestically with the endless northern horizon of snow-capped mountains.

Ahhh, this is the life. Open up a cool one for the master mariner, I directed the Mate, and one for yourself. And so, in utter contentment, we enjoyed the thrill of carefully threading our new yacht through the maze of freighters, tugs, fish boats, ocean liners and ferries in this mighty deep-sea harbor.

Soon the ocean's primeval push and shove took hold as we sliced through the tidal chop off Brockton Point; and then a feeling of awe engulfed us as we happily surrendered to the forces of nature and were swept serenely out to sea under the soaring span of the Lions Gate bridge in the tender embrace of a fast-ebbing tide.

You couldn't really call PUTZY TOO a Sangster boat. I don't think Bob approved of some of the changes I made to the designs he'd spent years developing.

I bought this PUTZY as a bare hull. By coincidence the price was exactly the same as the total in my bank account ! The boat was a standard production 22-foot fir-plywood planing hull with an 8-foot beam and a few interesting innovations. Bob had modified the bottom into a deep-V (like the Hatteras yachts) and fitted longitudinal steps like spray rails to ease the shock of driving into the waves.

My contribution had to do with the flare of the bow. In spite of the best efforts of fir-plywood design specialists like my friend marine architect John Brandelmayr, plywood boats at that time had a boxy look . . . the three-ply sheets could not take a compound curve to give a pleasing line.

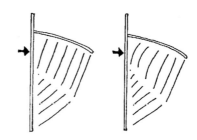

So on PUTZY we cut away part of the bluff bow and inserted thin, steam-limp mahogany planks to provide the double curvature of a voluptuous sheer line. Nothing really; why don't you do that on all your boats, Bob?

The cabin and flying bridge were standard pieces which Bob cut out for me in solid mahogany, from his patterns, and these I installed in the normal manner. Below I roughed in two V-berths, a small vanity-cum-storage locker and in the remaining corner, with a share of the main side window, the gleaming porcelain toilet in its own enclosed compartment.

That's where I made my first big mistake. There was ample room for the fixture and related plumbing, but not enough for the occupant under critical conditions. To put it bluntly, a man needs a fixed amount of room (unless he's double-jointed) to be able to pull his pants back up after sitting a-while. If there's not standing room (and there wasn't in PUTZY TOO's small head) then there must be extra space in which to bend forward. In my efforts to pack too much into too little, I positioned the forward bulkhead too damn close to the face of the sitee.

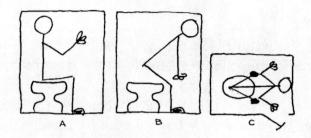

Thankfully, there was one way out . . . the large entry door to the head allowed a crabwise move out into the less-restricting space of the main cabin. But in this position your pants were slightly less than half-mast and the awkward exit invariably drew ribald laughter and jests from onlookers. Subsequent research revealed that women faced (?) the same problem. Which prompted one august CBC personality aboard to sing a few lines of the old ditty about the *naiveté* of a lass "who wore panties to a picnic."

My layout for the after end of PUTZY TOO was more successful. I left the cockpit large, for fishing and lazing about in. This was a good idea for it soon became apparent that this was the ideal place for the galley. Here I built a large, hinged table which folded down when not in use, with nearby stowage lockers for the Coleman camp stove, cutlery and crockery. A folding canopy top sheltered the cockpit from sun and rain and of course in the face of really inclement weather, everything could be set up below on a large countertop which covered built-in storage shelves.

Well, there's not much point in owning a yacht unless you can put to sea. It was summer holiday time and we were soon out on the briny, loaded to the Plimsoll with martinis, steaks, overdrafts and unlimited ignorance of things nautical.

Although we had spent many hours fishing local waters in the 18 months we owned the first PUTZY, those were short day trips for which that boat had been designed. Our one overnight cruise had been to a snug harbor about 10 miles from home base where we tied alongside a friend's 36-footer for dining and sleeping.

Now, however, we were self-contained and our cruising was limited only by the amount of time off I could wheedle from the boss, and we set forth in high spirits and completely oblivious to the many pitfalls which lay ahead. The first was close at hand.

A mere 30 nautical miles up the coast from Vancouver your Fearless Captain turned in to explore the several arms of Secret Cove, including the one beside Tom Ramsay's house which goes dry and nasty at half tide. Tom imparted this information at the top of his voice, in basic English, from the beach as I struggled to turn PUTZY TOO around in about a foot of fast-ebbing, rock-studded water.

"You bloody idiot," he roared for the whole bay to hear, "why don't you check your goddamn tide book?"

Hmmm.

With only a couple of bumps on the smooth rocks I managed to extricate PUTZY from this impossible channel, and swung in to Tom's wharf to thank him for the warning.

"Tie up here," he said gruffly, pointing to an empty space.

"With pleasure," I replied. "Come aboard and have a tot."

Tom knocked back the drink with practiced ease. I quickly poured him another and as he mellowed he explained the facts of life about local waters.

"just because this is an Island," he said, " it doesn't necessarily follow that you can sail around it when you please. You need water under your keel, and that's what tide books are for. Give me yours and I'll show you how to read it."

"Well, er, um, Tom, better have another drink. I don't think I have one aboard. Can I have a look at yours?"

13

"God almighty you're green. But you've landed at my wharf at a lucky time. An old Navy friend is coming for the weekend. Why don't you stay and join us? If we can't make you a sailor, we can at least drink you dry."

So naturally we did and besides picking up priceless (although often crudely-phrased) seafaring lore, we also experienced two of yachting's oldest maxims: the people you meet are more interesting than the places you visit; and, it's a bloody small world. Both these truths were exemplified by Tom and his wife Vivian, and his guests for the weekend, the Penn Taylor family from West Vancouver -- our next-door neighbors and very good friends.

⚓   ⚓   ⚓

There are many things to be learned before you can experience the utter contentment of life at sea.

For instance, after our first night aboard, anchored in an utterly peaceful cove, I was up at 5:30 wiping down the brightwork. Next day I rose at 7:30 and the next at 9:30. You see, it takes time to learn that all this rubbing wears away the varnish at an alarming rate. Only through superb will-power was I eventually able to remain in my bunk until the sun had effortlessly and efficiently dried the topsides.

Another early lesson involved the importance of frequent trips ashore to keep from becoming cramped in the small quarters aboard. In this, the dog was a great companion. As soon as I rose each morning, I found our corgi Punch eager to accompany me on the short row to the beach. Then I rowed us both back to the boat for breakfast. Soon it was ashore again with the dog; back for lunch; and then ashore again

for a longish spell just so His Nibs could inspect a few hundred acres of rainforest. And finally once again in the evening, for the night smells are vastly more interesting.

"You sleep well, the First Mate observed dryly. "You're doing nothing and yet you're tired."

"Dog-tired," I amended.

Overconfidence in seamanship must be avoided at all costs. My navigation skills, for instance, had been honed to perfection during years in the RCAF. I was especially proud of my map reading and delighted in recounting how I had flown through shot and shell in Europe during the war years with nothing between me and the safety of home base but a map of the world printed on my under-shorts.

The sparkling wine of boasting, however, suddenly turned sour the day we ran Putzy Too on the rocks in a serious way. I say "we" deliberately for of course I had an alibi. It was a small, rocky reef, unmarked and uncharted, in an area where the rest of the bottom was pure sand. (Which could be worse!) Whatever, we were stuck fast and the engine quit in disgust.

At this point the First Mate, who had been sharing lookout duties with the dog on the foredeck, turned to ask me why I had run onto the rocks. That raised my blood pressure to dangerous levels and triggered near-panic.

With my head full of square-rigger nonsense like "kedge her off" and other such tripe as I've written from time to time, I leapt into the dinghy completely forgetting that Johnny, the new outboard, could be restarted and was even provided with a reverse gear. However, by dint of furious sculling and repositioning the Mate and the dog to alter trim, I dragged PUTZY TOO off her first reef unharmed but not unscathed.

As I rested exhausted over the oars, a local nitwit appeared in a putt-putt and said: "Whatcha workin' for? Tide's coming in. You'd have floated off — easy — in a few minutes."

Other Captains have not been so lucky. My shipboard reading that weekend was a new book (Arctic Command) by my good friend Roland Wild in which Captain Thomas Smellie of the Hudson's Bay Company ship BAYRUPERT ran onto a rock and never did get off.

As I recall the story, Captain Smellie was sailing his supply ship up the Labrador coast en route to Hudson's Bay when, just like me, he ran onto an unseen (underwater) rock.

Did Smellie back off like me? No such luck. He measured 120 feet of water under the bow, and 150 feet under the stern, but amidships there was two feet of a pinnacle rock sticking up through the bottom of the ship right under the boilers. He had barely enough time to take to the boats before the ship foundered.

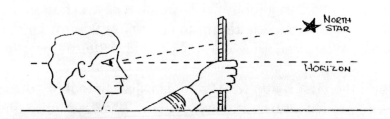

Navigation with compass or star was another skill with which I was wont to dazzle the natives. One prime demonstration occurred on PUTZY TOO.

We frequently cruised across the Gulf of Georgia, some 25 miles of open water which can blow up quickly into frightful proportions but at least you can usually see where you are going. On this particular day it was flat calm and a thick fog trapped us half-way across, limiting visibility to zero.

Well, this is what compasses are for I told the panicky crew. I'll just lay off a course on this here chart, which I had recently bought along with a tide book. To the dog's utter amazement I spread the chart over some gas cans which were cluttering the cockpit and measured our proposed course with a piece of taut string which I then freehanded over to the compass rose to read off the degrees. Not even forgetting the easterly variation in these parts.

If I say so myself, I have never set a truer course despite the fact that I had to steer with a tiny pocket compass, a rather inferior wartime souvenir. "Perfect landfall Skipper," the dog barked excitedly when he saw the harbor hove into view. Now that's real appreciation for emergency chart work.

Of course, any kind of accurate navigation depends on time — hours and minutes for measuring speed and distance, precise chronometers for calculations involving stars, and a standard point of reference. These basic requirements came together almost 200 years at the Royal Observatory at Greenwich on the Thames River near London, England, which I visited and wrote about some 50 years ago.

The first public time signal was instituted there in 1833 and consisted of dropping a black ball from one of the observatory turrets at one o'clock each day so that passing ships could set their chronometers.

But besides just having the correct time, navigators around the world needed a "place" against which to measure "noon" and figure out whether it was Tuesday or Wednesday wherever they happened to be.

This problem was resolved mainly through the efforts of a Canadian, Sanford Fleming, who proposed (in 1878) dividing the world into 24 standard meridians of longtitude which would form the basis for 24 different time zones. Greenwich, as a tribute to its prominence in the world of astronomy, was picked as the home of the prime meridian. An International Date Line — exactly half way around the world from Greenwich — was also established as the point where a day is either repeated or omitted by a traveller depending on whether he is going from the western to the eastern hemisphere, or vice-versa. This system quickly became an international standard as other countries began reckoning their local time from their distance, measured in meridians, from Greenwich.

At that point in history, the telegraph made its appearance and provided an easy way to transmit and correlate times in different areas. Then radio appeared which could transmit to ship's at sea, and soon everyone was enjoying a direct connection to Greenwich Mean Time (GMT).

At Greenwich, a battery of 18 quartz crystal clocks, working together and checking each other, broadcast the correct time continuously, even allowing for the time lag in transmission.

Those Greenwich clocks were more accurate timekeepers than the earth itself. Astronomical observations had long shown that the length of the day varies from time to time, and the clocks, which could split time into millionths, could indicate when those changes occurred.

Quite a few years ago, the Royal Observatory was moved from Greenwich to a country location away from the smog and air pollution of London which was ruining visibility of the heavens. The prime meridian , a line in the metal transit circle, remains at Greenwich, but just about everything else has changed. The current international standard time is now called Coordinated Universal Time (UTC) and is based on atomic clocks. These signals run our modern Ground Position Indicators, small computers which transmit precise navigation fixes from a series of satellites to anyone, anywhere on the globe.

I'm sorry to see the end of GMT, which I grew up with, mainly because it was tied in with the historic buildings at Greenwich and was thus so redolent of traditions of the sea. I'm not sure how the present day mariner indicates noon — presumably 1200 hours UTC. In the flying business we stick by an old nickname, as in 1200 hours Zulu.

⚓   ⚓   ⚓

Those first cruises about PUTZY TOO gave The First Mate, bless her, some difficult moments. One rainy evening I turned in early to fight off a sniffle. As I snuggled down with the Captain's Decanter within easy reach, the First Mate announced she would row the dog ashore for *his* nightcap. It was dusk already.

I woke suddenly an hour later. Out in the inky blackness which engulfed all creation came faint, plaintive cries: "Harry!" Harry!" There, in the pale beam of the flashlight I located the First Mate 50 yards astern, rowing stoutly but erratically, unable to catch up with PUTZY TOO as she skated smartly around the harbor on a long anchor line in the stiff breeze.

Up to this point it had never occurred to me that the Mate, a native of London's Mayfair, hadn't learned to row at the same time she learned to walk. "Pull on the right oar now on the left" I shouted across the water, and eventually she came alongside. Nothing to it really, when you're bred to the sea.

Katchoo !

The Good Old Days at Rivers Inlet (1956)

That damn phone just wouldn't stop ringing.

And the damn dog just wouldn't stop barking back at it.

I rolled over and squinted at the clock on the dresser — 4:30 in the morning for God's sake, although light was already brightening the eastern sky.

I finally crawled out of bed full of murderous thoughts, picked up the receiver and snarled, "Well, what is it, you bloody idiot? Don't you know it's the middle of the night?"

The cheerful laugh on the other end of the line identified my good friend Charlie, and his message sent me on wings of excitement to my 22-foot outboard express cruiser berthed at the West Vancouver Yacht Club. Soon I was pounding carefree through rough water on my way to a shipyard in North Vancouver for new engines, built-in gas tanks, transom well, water tanks . . . the works . . . plus a complete overhaul without regard to expense. All on Charlie's credit card!

Although this story took place more than 40 years ago, the details remain as fresh and exciting as ever.

I had launched my new boat PUTZY TOO a year earlier as a bare shell and had been frustrated ever since by lack of time and funds to finish her properly. Then suddenly, out of the blue, came Charlie's totally unexpected offer to make all my dreams come true. And I didn't even have to kill anybody !

This miraculous state of affairs arose from a magazine article I had written about Charlie Bradbury, the seed potato king hereabouts.

Charlie owned BRAD-WYNNE, sister ship to PUTZY TOO, and was one of the most enthusiastic and accomplished sports fishermen on the west coast.

For years he and his cronies had dreamed of a pilgrimage to the Shangri-La of salt water salmon — Rivers Inlet. There, in the glacial waters of a foggy fjord some 300 miles north of Vancouver, the world's largest salmon gathered in tantalizing thousands before running up the Owikeno, Kilbella and Chukwalla rivers to spawn.

World record catch on a rod a reel (then) was the 87-pound Tyee (big Spring salmon) by Vancouver hotel owner Frank Piscatelli. But commercial fishermen were said to have netted monsters over 100 pounds, which must have been almost as large as the blown-up photo of Frank's fish in the tap room of his hotel.

In 1955 Charlie couldn't stand it any longer. He pointed the bow of his new 22-footer north and to his intense surprise he and fishing pal Bill McWilliam arrived at Rivers Inlet alive ! Two more buddies arrived by air that evening and the next morning, at dawn, the quartet started getting fish...prime red Spring salmon, every one a Tyee...and weighing 39, 60, 42, 46, 47, 38, 42, 47,62 and 44 pounds.

Afraid the Good Lord might strike him dead if he didn't share this bonanza with less fortunate souls, Charlie asked me to publish his plans for a repeat trip in 1956 which would adopt convoy tactics if enough small boat owners wished to participate.

All hell broke loose when the story appeared in print. I don't know how Charlie found time to sell potatoes that year what with answering the mail, the phone and callers that besieged his small downtown office to talk fishing, particularly Rivers Inlet fishing.

In the 1950s, small sports fishing boats on the west coast were simple lapstrake skiffs with inboard air-cooled motors which putt-putted around calm local waters. Most hadn't even a cuddy to provide shelter from the rain. Outboard engines were small and cranky: the largest available was only 25 hp.

Stern drives had not been invented, nor small radars or fish finders. Fiberglass was being slowly introduced as a shiny white finish coat for fir plywood hulls.

And another thing — Rivers Inlet was a hell of a long way off, through waters in which few yachtsmen ventured even in medium-size craft of the day. There was absolutely no accommodation and very few services at Rivers which kept it the exclusive domain of the "big boat" yachtsman who could carry everything with him.

Flies, mosquitoes, bear and cougar made tenting unwise on the deltas at the river mouths. Along the shore the mountains rose so sharply from the water there were few level spots to set up camp. Some fresh water and fuel was available at the defunct canneries, but little else. During the brief season they provided wharves, sheds and convenience stores for the commercial fishermen. But they had usually shut down for the season by the time the mighty Tyee arrived and the fishing fleet had moved south with the salmon, along with the supporting packers and ice boats. Canning or storage/icing facilities for sports-caught fish were consequently as scarce as shear pins in the Gobi desert.

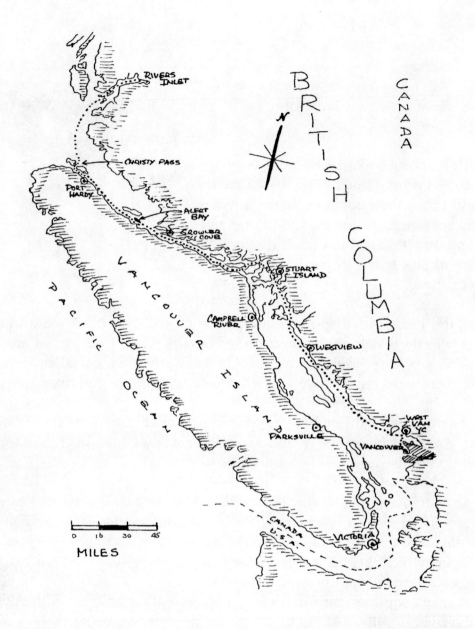

However, it takes more than a few hardships to dampen enthusiasm for a fishing trip and Charlie had already shown what was possible with the newly-developed 22-foot outboard cruisers. His own plywood boat, powered by twin Evinrude 25's, made 25 knots fully loaded. For his second trip he planned to install the latest 30 hp . engines to increase his speed and range. And for backup, he planned to hire a big seiner to escort the group across Queen Charlotte Sound, the largest expanse of open water on the trip.

24

Our group spent many exciting evenings debating these issues, and long hours plotting courses and compiling lists of supplies. Sleep was all but impossible in the heat of feverish anticipation. Whenever interest flagged, Charlie would pass around pages from his 1955 logbook:

". . . John hooked into a real large fish. He had 200 yards of line on his reel. The fish never stopped running . . . took all the line and tore up the outfit."

". . . Bill and Charlie hooked up with large fish at the same time. Fish crossed, badly tangling lines. Then they tangled with nearby fishermen. Finally when everybody's nerves were shot, Bill got his fish in the boat . . . 39 pounds.
"Charlie, still with his on, tangled his line around <u>both</u> outboard propellers. John, the lanky one, leaned way over to untangle it and Charlie finally landed the fish . . . 60 pounds."

Of course, Charlie kept saying that the biggest one got away, and pointed to this entry in his log book to "prove" it:

"Aug. 11 — Fish on all around us. John got a 44-pounder, Bill got one 60 pounds. Then John connected with a dandy and it towed us around for 45 minutes with no sign of giving up. All of a sudden up to the surface he came, made a tremendous swirl and roll, threw the hook and vanished. Estimated weight 90 pounds !"

True or false, it made tremendous reading although it pointed up the necessity of planning our visit for particular days to be assured of success, days which couldn't be calculated until late July when the big salmon actually arrived in the Inlet.

This wait-until-we-know timing problem thinned our group considerably. Quite a few keen members were already locked into firm holiday schedules dictated by family and job. Although small, our final flotilla — 4 boats, 11 men — made up for lack of size with boundless enthusiasm to battle the mighty Tyee.

Long age the Indians named the largest of the Spring salmon "Tyee," a word generally applied to fish weighing over 30 pounds. The Springs (more correctly called Chinooks) are the biggest of the five types of Pacific Coast salmon and despite their name run in the summer as do the others — Coho, Sockeye, Pinks, Chums.

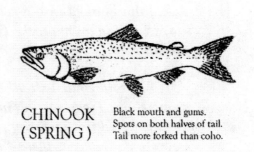

CHINOOK (SPRING)

Black mouth and gums.
Spots on both halves of tail.
Tail more forked than coho.

In Rivers Inlet the annual run of Springs was protected by special legislation and could only be fished by sportsmen under strict observation and control. That's why more than a thousand commercial fishermen who in a good year caught half a million Sockeye at Rivers had left before the sportsmen, and the Tyee, arrived.

Back in the 1920s there were more than 80 canneries operating on the B.C. coast with an average of 100 employees each during the fishing season. Originally the fish were salted, but they didn't keep well and had an odd taste. In cans, however, they could be preserved in prime condition for years.

Each cannery was a self-contained village with workplace, accommodation and stores for food and equipment which were open to all. It was estimated that these stores served a total of more than 10,000 people in coastal communities which consisted of loggers, sawmills, farmers and Indians, as well as the cannery workers. Supplies came from Vancouver on company boats or weekly steamships which made some 65 stops between Vancouver and Rivers Inlet.

Rivers Inlet Cannery where we would tie up courtesy of the Vancouver owners, was built in 1882 to process the fantastic Sockeye runs in the area which had been fished by the Owikeeno Indians for centuries.

It consisted of the abandoned cannery itself, plus housing for the staff and complete facilities for the fishermen such as net storage and repair floats, a store, fuel dumps, laundries and other conveniences.

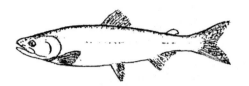

SOCKEYE   Large glassy eye. Almost toothless. Silvery sheen on body.

The fishermen themselves came from all over. They moved slowly southwards with the fish, delivering their catch each day to collector boats for a quick run to the nearest cannery for processing. In 1956 the fleet numbered some 3800 small (30-foot) gillnetters, 2800 slightly larger trollers and 450 purse-seiners which ran upwards of 50 feet. Total value of these 7000-plus vessels was $11 million and the total value of the gear and equipment they carried (including engines) was $90 million.

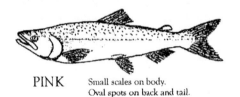

PINK   Small scales on body. Oval spots on back and tail.

CHUM   Slender wrist on tail. Faint bars on belly. Black edges on tail, anal and pectoral fins.

A commercial fisherman's precarious living fluctuated madly with the four-year life cycle of the salmon. In 1911 at Rivers Inlet, where there were about 18 canneries, fishermen received 10 cents a **fish** (sockeye). A bountiful harvest six years later brought more than twice as much. During the depression years, canneries were paying 2 cents a pound for Springs, and slightly more for other species. By way of comparison, in the 1990s fishermen received $2 a pound for fresh red Springs. Sockeye, the main fish for canning because it retains its appealing red color in the can, brought $3 a pound. The average Sockeye weighs around 5 pounds.

But these substantial figures didn't reflect the reality of life on the fishing grounds. Few commercial fishermen in those "good old days" owned their own boats outright. The great majority were deeply in hock to the fishing company, or just "rented" a boat from the company each season.

The fishing companies which owned the canneries dictated the rules. Rivers, at one point, was limited to 700 boats although there were 2,000 or more in surrounding areas. Large rowboats were common, as were sailing craft not much larger.

By the time we made our trip to Rivers in 1956, most of the B.C. canneries had been closed. Packers full of ice visited the fishing grounds to pick up daily catches for a newly-developed fresh fish market in towns and cities. Or they unloaded at a few centralized canneries near Vancouver which were serviced by rail and plane. Modern fishing vessels had developed on-board freezing facilities which made them much less dependent on coastal establishments. However, many canneries which had "closed " kept their floats and stores open during the season to service their company boats while in that particular area.

Charlie originally asked me along on the 1956 Rivers Inlet trip to provide transportation, accommodation and guiding for a couple of his Los Angeles business friends whose buying habits were closely related to their fishing success. When I pointed out that my PUTZY with a single 25 hp Johnson could only make nine knots compared to his 16, Charlie waved his hand airily and said:

"My friends will buy you a couple of new 30s, and fuel tanks, and all that. They've got millions. I'll be paying the other expenses. Now do you — or do you not — want to come to Rivers Inlet?"

I was stunned. Thousands of dollars worth of gear and motors just to take a couple of millionaires fishing. It couldn't be . . . and yet there was Charlie, impatiently awaiting an answer.

"Yes Sir, you've got yourself a boat, Charlie."

Actually the deal made sense, I told myself. Charlie's pals wanted the fun of the trip, a good boat to fish from, cheerful company and a snug berth at night. This PUTZY could provide, if I slept in the cockpit.

All it would take to make these two guys comfortable was money and they seemed to have plenty. Who was I to quibble over the chance of a lifetime?

So PUTZY was placed forthwith in the capable hands of North Vancouver shipwright George Bone to receive the fitting out of her young life. To strengthen the transom for the weight of another engine (two Johnson 30s were on order . . . the biggest they made) we decided to build a proper self-bailing motor well. For fuel, George devised tall, slim standup tanks which were bolted to the cockpit side of the cabin bulkhead. They look like small bureaux and had flat tops in case a chap wanted to put something down, like a glass.

Another refinement was an eight-gallon galvanized fresh water tank to replace a five-gallon can which had to be tipped to pour. The hinged tables in the cockpit where most of the cooking and washing was done were refined so that this area would be as clear as possible for fighting those world record salmon.

Even with those innovations, PUTZY had only the minimum facilities for the trip. The slightly-less-than-headroom cabin contained two built-in seven foot bunks forward, a six-foot galley cum dresser with stowage under, and an enclosed toilet. The windows were curtained, the mahogany gleamed with varnish, the ceiling and overhead were painted in harmonious shades of tan, electricity and water was laid on, and a place provided for (almost) everything. Modest as she was, PUTZY had cost me about $50,000, figuring my time (after the shipyard finished) at a nickel an hour.

Our evening gatherings continued apace as our group computed courses, tallied supplies and listed endless details. We drastically reduced our original lists of grub. Charlie found last year that everywhere he stopped for gas there were well-stocked stores. This means we would be traveling lighter, as well as faster. To be sure, Charlie added two new blue Evinrude 30s to BRADWYNNE.

We also included an exhaustive review of life-saving equipment, fire extinguishers, first aid kits, charts, spare parts, emergency gear . . . the limitless minutiae that makes boating so absorbing. And it wasn't all indoors camaraderie. Our group fished local waters several times together, just getting acquainted, and I quickly realized my new friends were quintessential professionals.

As the time for departure neared, the most stunning thing of all happened. Charlie phoned me quite casually one day to say that his two friends couldn't make the trip after all. . . they were flying to South America to fish marlin !

Ye Gods, PUTZY all dressed up and nowhere to go. I'd carried out my part of the arrangement, buying everything to get her ready. And Charlie had certainly carried out his part by paying for it all ! I kept wondering when I would wake up. Charlie must figure to write this off as a business expense, or else the price of seed potatoes is going to take a hell of a jump.

At any event, he didn't seem worried. He was absolutely all heart and determined to have PUTZY a member of the fleet. In the end he suggested I take his good friend Wright Chappell of New Westminister, a long-time sports fishing enthusiast, and I excitedly put the final supplies aboard.

A test run around the harbor with the new 30s showed PUTZY planing easily now about 20 knots. Most exhilarating after the slow displacement speeds I had been used to. Northside Marine had done a fine job of work and PUTZY was indeed ready for those two millionaires — Chappell and Furniss.

⚓   ⚓   ⚓

On Saturday Aug 4 I arrived on board at 0430 hours to find Wright, whom I hadn't met before, sacked in as if he owned the ship. Conscious of the huge sum it had cost Charlie to make Wright this comfortable, I thought I'd whip up a decent breakfast to start us off properly. In truth, I was so excited that I needed something to eat before I fell apart. Eggs, toast and coffee were on the table in a trice. Wright looked kind of stunned at this service. What the hell, hasn't he ever seen a fellow-millionaire before?

Soon Wright was dressed, the dishes done, our gear stowed and PUTZY looked the shippiest of her life. When Charlie arrived from Coal Harbor, he suggested that as PUTZY had only two men aboard, we should carry the spare 25 hp outboard. So we stowed this in the cabin between the bunks. From one to three engines in a week — not bad.

At 0530 hours we shoved off, four of us in loose formation: Commodore Bradbury in BRADWYNNE led the fleet with crew of Bill McWilliam, the ship chandler from C.P.Leckie, and John Douglass, a sales rep with Monsanto. All three were AAs and they must have been carrying at least a hundred jugs of their favorite brew — grapefruit juice. In AMIGO were Jack Birch and his two young sons; and in MANIDOVER were Roly Neale (Manitoba Hardware), Russ Gennest (Dover Transport) and Bill Matterson (Lions Gate Bridge).

We clipped off the miles northward with effortless ease. Cowans Point 0555 hours; Gower Point 0635; White Islets 0700; PUTZY riding softly about 16 knots, a couple under her maximum.

Got out the fishing rods off Cape Cockburn to pick up a coho for lunch while AMIGO went into Pender Harbor to refuel.

The rest of us made Westview easily. Chap high above on the steamer wharf lowered the nozzle of a long, oily hose as we fended off the barnacle-encrusted piles. PUTZY took 18 gals of gas/oil.

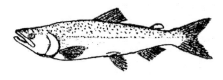

COHO   Black tongue, white gums.
        Only top half of tail is spotted.

31

Sarah Point 1300 hours; Bullock Bluff 1410; Stewart Island 1500 for a second refueling at a proper small-boat float. Sunny, light chop, refreshing breeze. Sparkling blue sea. Ever-changing view as the islands passed and we gazed up the reaches of unknown bays and inlets. Bill Mac had all the charts and was navigating for the fleet.

We ran through the Yaculta Rapids at high slack and then stopped to turn over the spare motor to AMIGO. Minutes later stopped again to help them with plug trouble. Johnstone Strait was quite sloppy but we made several more stops to tinker with AMIGO's engine. Even with three motors, she didn't fancy our company.

Aboard PUTZY things were running like clockwork. Wright turned out to be an ideal shipmate — a former tugboat skipper and present shipyard owner. He was a convivial type, busy celebrating his 50th birthday, and was equally happy hoisting a toast (to himself) or spending spare time tickling up the engines or whipping lines.

While I was below cooking up dinner, Wright, at the helm, poked his head through the hatch and hollered how great it was to be in Johnstone Strait where at last we were free of deadheads. At that instant we ran right over the granddaddy of them all -- a 60-foot hemlock log that kicked up both motors but luckily nothing else. Fortunately I was holding the pots on the stove because of the choppy water so our dinner didn't hit the deck. In the evening the sea flattened out and we coasted, dog-tired, into Growler Cove at dusk.

I couldn't help but admire the way Wright coped with life on a small craft. After all, he's a boat builder who normally scorned anything under 50 feet on the waterline, or with less power than a 500 hp Enterprise diesel. Unless he had at least three solid inches of decking under his feet, he was uncomfortable.

I had tried to cheer him up earlier as we pounded along in the Johnstone Strait chop, after clipping that deadhead.

"For Heaven's sake Wright, stop worrying. We've got real solid stuff under us -- three-eighths of an inch of fir plywood !"

He winced, and then started casually examining the cockpit coaming.

"This is loose," he said. "That's why she leaks in the rain. Hand me a wrench and I'll tighten up the through bolts."

"The what bolts ?"

"Through bolts. What do you think holds this in place ?"

"But Wright," I protested, "this is a small pleasure boat ... I built the whole damn thing and I never even heard of a through bolt. Good old bronze screws hold that coaming on, and each screw is under a wooden plug and each wooden plug was put in by my wife with her own little hands ... 999 mahogany plugs, each tapped and glued into place. If you think I'm going to break out a couple and ruin the varnish just because you want to tighten things up, you're nuts."

Poor Wright. He winced again and I could sense a yearning for his Lulu Island boatyard where a timber was a timber was a timber -- 12 x 12 x 12.

The next morning we were off at 0645 in heavy sea fog. Our fleet navigator gave us slips of paper with compass courses in case we became separated. Refueled in Alert Bay and took the spare motor back from AMIGO which would stay there and try and rectify chronic engine trouble. MANIDOVER was having trouble, too. Roly had the only Mercury engines in the fleet and they kept demanding freshly- cleaned plugs.

By noon we were at Christie Pass and Charlie was once again handing around his credit card as we refueled. Around the point was the open Pacific and we were anxious about the next 40 miles across Smith Sound. The commercial fishermen gather here in nervous clusters to wait for favorable weather before pressing on although they are well accustomed to being out alone day and night in the foulest weather.

The wharfinger said a large gaggle of boats had left at dawn, going north, so we assumed that the fine weather would at least hold for us.

Still, it was with some trepidation that we poked out and for the first time picked up the powerful ocean swells. In these large rollers the boat alongside disappears completely from sight in the trough which made for some interesting photography. However the sun was brilliant, the sea calm and the wind light, and we tore along in high spirits.

Off Cape Caution schools of dolphin joined us to frolic in the foaming bow waves. Perhaps these always-smiling dolphins are trying to tell us something. They are friendly air-breathing mammals which scientists think we may eventually be able to talk to. They have a large, well-developed brain (which is why they can be so easily trained in aquariums) and "talk" to each other in the forms of squeaks, whistles and barks. They also have a highly-developed sonar system which bounces a clicking noise off obstacles ahead in the path of travel.

But there is bad news, too — dolphins (all-same porpoise) are members of the whale family and close cousin to the killer (pilot) whales. They have a mouth full of needle-sharp teeth and eat 15-20 pounds of salmon a day !

We ran past Pine Island and Egg Island and finally reached the haven of Rivers Inlet, the mouth protected by a group of islands. We stopped to strip cast the kelp beds there but were too keyed up to take our work seriously. Time was flitting by, so we carried on up the Inlet about which we had dreamed and talked so much. Running near the shore we saw deer, and a bear, and then a most discouraging sight . . . a dozen or so giant killer whales. When these blackfish are around, the salmon aren't. They drive everything in the ocean wild with fear and kill any chances of sport fishing for up to 24 hours. The Indians claim the flesh of these ravenous carnivores has a rich flavor and they consider it quite a delicacy. Small consolation.

Some fishermen have been known to bang away at blackfish with 30-30s, but the shots don't seem to have much effect. Even though the big whales can ruin fishing for days on end, it's a hell of a way to treat them.

Continuing up this interminable inlet (it was only about 30 miles but we were tired after two full days) we overhauled the 60-foot PRIDE OF THE WEST under charter to some of Wright's pals from the Marpole Rotary Club. We sped close alongside and after exchanging friendly insults, hurled them a dead cod.

Finally, at the head of the inlet, we checked in with the special fisheries officer, got our permits and tied to the Rivers Inlet Cannery net float where we slept like the dead in utter peace.

Up early the next morning. It was August 6 and the big salmon had arrived; all we had to do was catch them. Started trolling at 0630 quite close to the beach. But soon a school of blackfish came blowing up the opposite shore a mile away. We couldn't expect much luck with these whales around, but we'd come too far not to fish.

By 1000 hours we were trolling off the old Kildala Cannery near the mouth of the big river. Reminded us of home when a small rental skiff crossed our bow with **SEWELL** (of Horseshoe Bay) painted on the side. A large yacht had brought several along as tenders.

At 1045 I replaced my large brass Gibbs spoon with a plastic Pintail plug. These white and red plugs weren't yet on the market yet but my good friend Pintail had given a few to "experts" for testing. They closely resembled the traditional Luckie Louie plug, but had "Pintail differences" which he claimed would make them deadly. Pintail was naturally anxious for a report on his plug's effectiveness but I'd been trolling one around Howe Sound for some time without success.

"Maybe it's waiting to show its magic at some appropriate place — like Rivers, " I told Wright.

"And if Pintail's name on the plug doesn't catch us a fish, we're still even with everybody else around here," he answered cynically.

Returned to the cannery for lunch and gas and were out fishing again soon, but a stiff "afternoon" chop was building up. Sunny. Ran the motors two hours each; no oiling at trolling speed. Besieged by millions of biting (stinging) horseflies. (Deerflies?) Knocked off after a total of 10 hours fishing for the day. A good try but the blackfish jinx held true.

Next morning we were at it again bright and early. Just when we were ridiculing "that bloody fool over there with a child's bait-casting rod," he hit into something. This big oaf was sharing a tiny dinghy with another huge chap. We wondered cynically how they stayed afloat, and mercilessly criticised the fishermen, their boat, their gear, their ancestors, but our jokes petered out quickly when the idiot one boated a salmon about 20 pounds.

Several other fishermen with similar gear were bobbing around. Probably Americans who traditionally fancy those short rods with geared-down reels mounted upside down so they could keep a thumb on the line.

Light rain started as we were breakfasting and trolling the far side of the inlet. No sign of blackfish, yet. No flies, either, since we invested in a three-dollar anti-bug spray-bomb at the cannery store. But no-see-ums galore. Swat. Swat.

Out fishing again after tea, and the usual afternoon blow. Bill Matterson rumored to have boated a 44-pounder but no action in our area. Some of the boys took the afternoon off to hunt out-of-season willow grouse in the marsh. *Tsk. Tsk.*

At 1915 Wright tied into something. Very heavy, but definitely not bottom. Hook broke free after two minutes of indecisive action. No marks on it, or kelp or weeds. Think we may have lost a big one due to impatience setting the hook.

"Fish for dinner at last," cried Charlie as we got home after dark. Bill had indeed landed a big one and Charlie was overjoyed to see some positive return on his large investment in this safari. Although we stuffed ourselves, there was still plenty to share with other boats.

Blackfish have ruined the fishing for days now. Boats that were here long before us were still jinxed. Although the whales didn't show today, we decided that if they reappear tomorrow we'll push off for Bute or Knight Inlets where the salmon may not be quite as large, but where we should be able to catch them.

"You know, we're lucky aboard PUTZY," said Wright. "The other boats each have *three* guys bitching and binding all the time."

The killer whales had snorted up the shores of Rivers Inlet each morning for nine consecutive days. They traveled on schedule and cruised in schools up both shore lines promptly at 0800 hours,

scaring the living hell out of everything else in the water. They're ferocious monsters about 30 feet long and weigh tons. In spite of rumors they don't attack boats or people. But they're a lot bigger than PUTZY and we stayed well clear.

Time passed quickly, what with cooking meals, cursing flies and gnats, having the odd drink, running the boat, visiting around.

John David Eaton the department store tycoon was there in his 90-foot HILDUR. H.R. MacMillan the lumber baron was there in his 140-foot MARIJEAN (on which I was to spend some time, years later, as First officer) with a deck load of crumbling Queen Charlotte Island totem poles for restoration in Vancouver. There was a 100-footer from New York; and airplanes, dinghies and other craft in great profusion as us millionaires lived it up. Several boats had left to try fishing other places, including Tom Ramsay and party aboard SMUGGLER and his son Dana's charter boat WHITE ARROW.

We enjoyed meeting the friendly characters on one nearby yacht. Wright had built this twin-diesel 42-foot bridge-deck cruiser for a pal some years earlier and went slightly mental every time he saw her because the owner had insisted the height of the amidships saloon be raised out of proportion.

Before dawn, after a rather full night of partying, this cruiser pulled out from a berth near us. Wright and I were washing up in the cockpit as she slid by only a few feet off in the clammy mist. From her flying bridge a loud-hailer vented mournful howls . . . Roly Dean, irrepressible even at this hour, masquerading on the flying bridge in a rubber werewolf face mask !

The HILDUR, owned by John David Eaton, the department store chap, was tied up across the float from PUTZY. Those large net floats had 2x4 rails at intervals over which the fishermen drape their nets while they repaired the mesh or tied on new corks and leads. When HILDUR came in, several white-jacketed hands leapt smartly to the float and hitched lines around these light posts. On instructions from the magnificently-uniformed professional captain, the engines surged ahead to bring the yacht alongside against her spring lines.

But of course what happened was that post after post snapped off as the big yacht moved relentlessly down the float. Eventually the Captain changed tactics in the face of a loudly-shouted barrage of advice from the rest of us on the float. Don't know what made him so touchy. We were only trying to help.

One thing about HILDUR that particularly caught my eye were her large white canvas-bag fenders. When she went out for a run in the afternoon, I "borrowed "one which had been left behind and tied it to the wharf beside PUTZY to check its efficiency. When I got back that night it had been "borrowed" back. I tried again the next day but lost it again. Eaton is a tough man to shoplift.

Eventually the skipper got over his snit and invited us aboard HILDUR for a look around. Wright had mentioned he was particularly interested in the engine room. (Four diesels on two shafts, as I recall it.) We had a most instructive tour — dutifully tugging our forelocks as we passed through the owner's quarters — and ended up in the magnificently-equipped wheelhouse.

As the Captain pointed out the radar, the loran, the echo sounders and the rest, I could hear violins accompanying his polished recital and realized that this was the song he enjoyed singing to guests in dinner jackets who didn't know the blunt end from the sharp end.

When the Captain , a kindly guy really, started reeling off the rules of the road in verse, I was afraid Wright (the rugged tugboat captain) would tear up the polished brass binnacle and ram it down that melodious but patronizing throat.

⚓   ⚓   ⚓

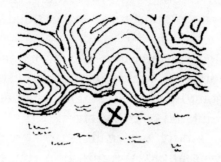

Wednesday August 8 turned out to be my lucky day:

- 0530 hours started fishing
- 0610 fish on
- 0710 fish aboard ... 59 1/2 pounds !

I was up exceptionally early that morning, spurred by Bill's success of the previous day. I told Wright to grab a few extra winks below while I took PUTZY a mile or so along the shore to a special piece of water that we fancied.

There I shut down one engine, slowed the other to trolling speed, got the two rods rigged and clamped in their holders. I had just ducked back into the cabin to set up the stove for breakfast when the Tyee struck.

Very heavy at first, and not much action. It could have been bottom — we were only a dozen yards off the beach. But it didn't *feel* like bottom, although the line went out slowly as PUTZY's momentum carried her ahead. Shoved the motor out of gear and applied pressure on the line. Then, when nothing seemed to be happening, I banged the rod butt vigorously with my fist . . . an old Pintail tactic . . . and the fish took off for a scorching 200-yard sprint.

As the line melted off the reel at an alarming rate, I realized we'd have to follow the fish or he'd break me before I could get him turned around. About six things needed doing at once and I desperately needed Wright . . . *but I couldn't remember his damned name !*

So there I stood, rod in one hand, line screaming off into the dawn; Wright's rod in the other hand, trying to reel it in so it wouldn't foul my line or the propellers; trying to re-start the engine which I had stalled in the initial excitement; trying to steer PUTZY which was drifting dangerously close to the rocks; and all I could think to holler down into the cabin was "Hey, *you !* Hey *you !*" at my sleeping partner. The uproar — or maybe the lack of engine noise — finally roused Wright who came pelting up into the chill dawn in his under shorts. Between us we got the other line in, the motor going again, and turned PUTZY to follow the fish. Not a second too soon . . . I had lost 200 yards or more of 30-pound test line and was well into the 100 yards of backing. And the salmon didn't seem the slightest bit interested in stopping his run.

Eventually I got the fish turned and as he came towards the boat, I managed to pick up some badly-needed slack. Then, with a bit in reserve and Wright steering the boat in his underwear, I sat back to pay a patient game. I let the salmon run all he wanted, keeping a fair amount of tension on the line. In fact, on some of his longer runs, he noticeably towed PUTZY along too. With such a light line, and a leader of about 20 pounds, there wasn't much else I could do except tire him out thoroughly, and I impatiently sweated out Pintail's formula for the big ones . . . a minute a pound.

Almost to the hour I had the powerful deep-bellied salmon alongside, panting but not yet exhausted and over on his side, although he'd been going about four knots for 55 minutes.

The sight of the boat sent him off on several furious dashes, but each one was shorter than the last. After our first look at the big fish, Wright and I kept our fingers crossed for he seemed to be hooked by only one prong of the leading treble hook and the metal — to say nothing of his mouth — must be suffering under the strain.

Slowly I worked him closer and closer, with Wright taking a lot of the strain by skillful maneuvering of PUTZY. I was shaking with excitement, and tension, and fatigue, when the moment finally came for Wright to lean cautiously over the side with the landing net.

He must have been shaking too, for he tangled the damn net in the other triple-prong hook which was dangling free from the Pintail plug an inch off the salmon's snout. The fish, which wouldn't fit into the net anyway, seemed to realize that the battle wasn't lost, and with one enormous shake of his head, broke the only prong of the hook that was holding him.

That final grand gesture, however, took his last ounce of strength and he lay panting on the surface, free as the breeze but too damn spent to flick his powerful tail and escape.

"The gaff . . . the gaff . . . " Wright shouted frantically, still struggling to free the net.

"Forgot to bring it," I replied.

"Come on, then, " he urged and in unison we leaned over the high gunnel and hanging by what must have been our toenails, grabbed the fish with bare hands. Wright jammed as much of the tangled net as he could over the fish's head and got a hand in his gills, while I settled for a two-handed grip on the huge slippery wrist. With one great heave we brought a very startled salmon aboard.

The relief was like champagne. We spent the next two hours babbling congratulations to each other, and telling passing boats how we picked the big boy off the edge of the kelp on a dry fly. There was no fooling about his weight, though; we checked him in, as required, at the Fisheries station and had him recorded officially at 591/2 pounds, length 45 inches, age four years, male, the 156th fish to be taken at Rivers that year.

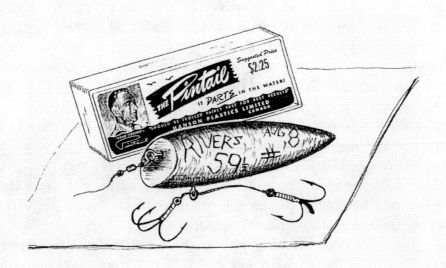

And we took photos, lots of photos. Wright snapped me holding the fish; I snapped Wright holding the fish. The Fisheries Officer snapped me, and Wright, and both of us. We photographed that lovely Tyee from a dozen different angles and I was especially careful as I unloaded the films and tucked them away in my breast pocket.

"OK ,Wright, " I said. "Fresh film is in the camera. Let's go get *your* Tyee."

So saying, I jumped down to the wharf and bent over to untie PUTZY's lines. As I did, the two rolls of film slipped quickly and cleanly out of my shirt pocket and disappeared in the salt chuck. *For God's sake ... my finest catch and not even a picture !*

By this time the Fisheries Officer had gutted the Tyee for inspection and had taken out the gills. We dressed up the empty sagging belly and gap around the head with fishhooks as best we could and took some more photos, but the pristine beauty of my original trophy had gone. As well as the sun and the final effort was just deep shadows. Hence the sketch.

Fish were being played all over the Inlet as we resumed trolling. This was the second day the blackfish had stayed away and the difference was noticeable.

By lunchtime John Douglass had boated a 55-pounder and Bill McWilliam a 56-pounder. Rivalry between our boats grew keener and Wright fretted visibly as the day ended without another strike aboard PUTZY.

That evening I spent hours trying to get on the cannery radio telephone but the airways were jammed with commercial traffic. I knew Pintail would be delighted to hear about my fish, the largest ever on his new plastic plug, and would want to run the story in his column in The Province. When I finally managed to get through to Vancouver there was no answer.

This was doubly annoying, for there was another point that Pintail would have liked to hear. My fish had taken the lure at exactly 0610 hours which was the beginning of the major solunar period for that day. These tables, devised by John Alden Knight and published weekly in many newspapers, are closely related to tides and have long intrigued sportsmen.

Or perhaps it should be the other way around — the effect of the tides (and of course the moon) on the feeding habits of wildlife have long intrigued the sportsman. Pintail and I had had long discussions about these tables which delineate favored times and generally agreed that while most of us had to take our fishing and hunting when we could manage it, we would certainly pick a solunar period in preference to any other time if it was at all possible.

Sadly, the reason Pintail wasn't at home that evening to hear my excited chatter was that he just been rushed to hospital with what proved to be a fatal heart attack. I saw him briefly the day we got back to Vancouver but he was failing fast. He shook my hand with amazing strength and said from the depths of his plastic oxygen tent: "Henry, get me out of here."

Wish to God that I could, but all I managed to answer was, "You'll be out soon, in plenty of time for the (fall) steelhead." But it didn't work out that way and he died soon after. If there's fishing to be enjoyed in the next world, gentlemen like Pintail certainly deserve to be first rod on the pool at dawn.

My dear old friend Pintail loved nothing more than to clown in front of the camera to make a serious point. Here his rubber face and sense of humor signals the approach of the hunting season , and the caution that Guns and Alcohol don't mix.
Photo by Chuck Jones, The Province.

44

The next morning we set out in the dark to catch Wright's Tyee. It was August 9 and our last few hours at Rivers. News of my fish and many other good catches had the whole inlet feverish with excitement.

By 0530 the shoreline was thick with RAY's BOATS from a Seattle rental firm which had been brought up in bulk on a scow for the swarms of sportsmen who were now turning up on large yachts or seaplanes. More than 100 fishermen were concentrated along one productive but short piece of shoreline at 0700 hours. They were fishing out of everything from six-foot dinghies to a 160-footer registered in Miami.

Charlie picked up a 50-pounder about 0800. Lots of Coho jumping off the mouth of the Owikeno river, but we want to concentrate on the Tyees. Only about three hours were left before we would have to head south. We'd even used up the spare hours held in reserve in case bad weather delayed our progress home.

Wright and I just *knew* we could fill the boat sometime that day, but time was against us and although by general agreement we stretched and re-stretched the departure hour, eventually we had to reluctantly reel in, pick up gas and the spare motor, and leave.

The week, which had once seemed more than enough to fulfill our dreams, had suddenly turned out to be far too short. Bad weather was forecast and a quick departure was prudent.

Down the inlet, opposite the mouth of Moses Inlet, we managed a last-ditch troll in a particularly fishy looking spot, but our luck had run out. We stopped to ice down the two fish aboard BRADWYNNE at Wadhams, but without much hope of getting them home in the summer heat without spoiling. A stiff breeze and vigorous chop built up as we neared the mouth of Rivers Inlet and we wondered if we had left it too late.

As we started to pick up the ocean swell, my stomach twinged with unease. No wonder -- we were all bloated from eating salmon the night before which we couldn't take home with us. We gave away at least 30 pounds of choice cuts to a forest survey crew which arrived out of the hills at a most fortunate moment . Neighboring fishermen didn't want any ... they had too much of their own. It broke my heart to see so much thrown away -- I kept thinking of my wife's relatives in England buying those teeny-weeny little cans at a dollar each!

Eight men, of course, couldn't do justice to the 300 pounds of prime red salmon our group had caught in one day. Heaven knows we tried, though.

Aboard PUTZY it was Wright's turn to cook, and he gave me a boastful resume of his prowess. He had very definite opinions on just how salmon steaks should be done and bubbled with enthusiasm as he prepared to mess up every pot and pan aboard, knowing full-well that he who cooks does *not* do the dishes.

"The big secret with salmon," he explained, "is to get the pan really hot and then sear the fish, sealing in the juices like a steak."

"You're the chef," I said. "And we've certainly got plenty of fish to experiment with."

Wright looked hurt, and muttered darkly "you'll see" as he cut a couple of steaks that must have gone two pounds each and wouldn't come near to fitting in the pan. "You'll see," he repeated as he checked the heat of the pan with a drop of water which sailed off like a pistol shot, and then slid the first piece of fish in. A cloud of fat globules sprayed everything for a hundred yards around and I couldn't help protesting.

"Nonsense," said Wright. "Just keep the pan good and hot and you can't go wrong."

As he prodded the fish with a spatula a nostril-twitching aroma of sizzling salmon engulfed us. Absolutely tantalizing. By the time Wright declared the steak ready for the table I was drooling all over my T shirt and banging the table with my cutlery in uncontrollable impatience.

With a smug flourish, Wright slithered the steak onto my plate. I stabbed voraciously into the golden-rich surface and shoveled in a mouthful worthy of the original starving Armenian. *Christ, it was awful!*

"For God's sake Wright, it's raw," I spluttered, spitting out a large piece.

"The outside looks good," he said.

"Why sure, you numbskull, but this damn steak is two inches thick and the inside is absolutely untouched by heat."

"Don't shout," said Wright. "We'll do you another. Fussy son of a bitch."

And he nonchalantly threw two pounds of prime red salmon over the side and put another steak in the pan which by now had cooled some.

This one was cooked to perfection and when I had finished he fixed himself one, and another two which we could have cold tomorrow.

As we rolled into bed that night with skins like salamis, I couldn't help belching that I didn't really have the stomach for the life of a millionaire sportsman.

And, Oh Boy, those damn dirty dishes!

We stopped that night at Duncanby Landing to see if the weather would let up for the run across the open water. Our cardinal rule was to wait rather than rush.

It was pleasant there, among small islands near the mouth of Rivers inlet. Charlie told the affable storekeeper that he wasn't selling enough potatoes. *Nobody* sells enough potatoes, says Charlie, but then he's in the business. The storekeeper's home was along the shore a hundred yards or so and we heard that when you become friends you may be invited along to share a musical evening which centres around a magnificent electric organ.

Before dark we visited nearby Goose Bay cannery, and then trolled around although rough water rolling in from the open Pacific made it unpleasant. No rain, but Wright felt it was in the offing and rubbed the inside of the windshield with tobacco from a broken cigarette so that it wouldn't fog up. Bull Durham was the best for that, he contended, but he was fresh out.

During Wright's trick at the wheel I amused him by reading the book of instructions that came with the new Johnson outboards. To my amazement, and Wright's annoyance, I discovered why we had been plagued by stiff steering this whole trip in spite of his considerable monkey wrenching. A simple swivel tension screw was set up too tightly.

Marine weather reports early the next morning were not encouraging, but the general feeling was that we should give the open water a try. Fog patches, light breeze, heavy swell , engines rough -- great time for *them* to develop personalities. The water looked nasty but the others pushed ahead so we followed. Steering 250 degrees, then 160 for Egg Island.

Gone were the sparkling blue wavelets and the acrobatic dolphins of the trip up. A determined southwesterly was blowing against the tidal outflow from Smith Inlet and the result was frightful. PUTZY's pounding engines threatened to disappear from view as large seas rolled up astern. It was exhilarating to race down the face of the waves but steering control virtually disappeared and broaching became a real danger.

Bill McWilliam was navigating for us all, as usual. But fearing we might become separated in the poor visibility, he passed out cards with courses and times computed to Christie Pass, some 40 miles off across open water.

BRADWYNNE carried the master set of large detailed charts where Bill could work on them, and the rest of us could look them over during refueling stops. This system worked well on the way up, and we made our landfalls on time. But in between, we never knew exactly where the hell we were.

Off Egg Island the skies were even blacker, if that was possible. A heavy swell was kicking up and cresting. Putzy was running full blast, though, on 142 degrees for Pine Island. Off Cape Caution at 0655 hours in an unpleasantly confused sea. Sky threatening but wind still light. PUTZY roller-coasting in the heavy swells.

Red storm-warning flags were flying at Pine Island and the seas became alarming. A startling crash below signalled that crockery was adrift. Wright disappeared to check, and try and figure out something for breakfast. A minute later he emerged with a half-glass of rye.

"Here's some orange juice to start breakfast off," he said, solemnly toasting the gyrating horizon. We'd been out of grog for days, but Wright had somehow secreted a bottle ... no mean feat on a crowded 22-footer.

The warmth of that raw whisky was just what Nelson would have ordered for a morning like this. I handed my empty glass to Wright who disappeared below "to fix up some bacon and eggs."

A moment later he was back again, with another big shot of rye. "Only way to do bacon and eggs in rough water," he explained. Then, after a few minutes he asked, "toast?"

"Why not," I said, and we had another drink. The toast was particularly tasty, so we had a second order, and then topped "breakfast" off with a side order of strawberries, I think.

By this time it was blowing at least a gale, but somehow it didn't seem to matter much. We felt quite brave shutting down the engines in that horrendous jumble of water to bat kelp off the propellers with a paddle. Man, that's boating!

A proper breakfast and walk ashore at sheltered Christie Cove started the day off again . . . this time more soberly . . . and we set off down Blackfish Sound in a ripple compared with the morning's open ocean run. Wright sat in the sun and carved the date of my big catch on the Pintail plug.

In retrospect the whole trip was a bit more than the casual 600 miles I had written about so enthusiastically. When I airily dismissed most of the route as "inside" or "protected" waters, a lot of old-timers on the coast must have chortled. Some stretches of water, viewed from the bouncing bridge of PUTZY looked positively frightening at times. Even during "breakfast."

A 22-footer is an awfully frail cockle when you get out on the toughest coastline in the world. Thank God boat and motors were in perfect shape before we started.

But just when we began to feel like heroes, Roly Deane of Marpole passed us in a l4-foot runabout. I guess you could make the trip in a bathtub (as one chap tried to do later) if you could wait for the right weather and were slightly mad to start with.

At Port Hardy we stopped to see Roly Neale off by plane. As luck would have it, Wright found a tavern and thoughtfully picked up some beer. It was a tossup who drove and who snoozed down Johnstone Strait that afternoon.

The locals lounging on the Hardy wharf were highly amused at the way Wright tied PUTZY up. As befits an old tugboat hand, he brought her in fast, killed way with a huge burst of reverse, and then before she had even stopped ran down the wharf to sling a bowline around the nearest bollard, letting wind and tide hold PUTZY off the wharf while he went for the beer. Fenders and stern lines are for amateurs!

Soon off again down Blackfish Sound in a moderate chop, PUTZY crew happily working on the beer. First mishap of the trip -- a broken shear pin --occurred off Pultney Point.

Bill McWilliam tied BRADWYNNE stern-to and replaced it for us. These long shafts are *long* when you have to reach out to the prop.

Refueled at Alert Bay and continued southward. In the afternoon the wind increased again and soon frothed up trouble in lower Johnstone Strait. Where the wind and tide run against each other off Helmcken Island, a nasty confused chop can build up in minutes. No alternative but to keep PUTZY pounding through it, although for the first time that day I had a twinge of apprehension.

With difficult seas, my inclination was to ease back on the throttle as we'd race down the back of a large crest before crashing into the wall of water at the bottom of the trough. But Wright kept urging full throttle and didn't seem at all concerned until PUTZY took an exceptionally vicious lurch which tossed him out of his bunk.

At times like that you realize the inadequacies of a planing hull. In spite of a deeply-cut forefoot, PUTZY had lots of virtually flat bottom for speed, which in rough water slammed down with shuddering crashes which tested every fastening as well as our teeth. The wide, flat stern made quartering all but impossible, and broaching a distinct possibility. Thank God for the new self-bailing motor well — it kept many a gallon of water out of the cockpit that day.

Finally we rounded Althorp Point, battered and bruised but still alive, and then whistled through an almost too-active Wellbore Rapids. Hit the Green Point rapids on high slack water, and tied up in Shoal Bay for the night.

Onward the next morning through the Yuculta Rapids on high slack. John Douglass of BRADWYNNE was aboard PUTZY for this lap and his knowledge of the reef south of Savary Island proved valuable as we worked our way into the shallow water to stripcast for Coho.

Here Wright finally came into his own, and boated five fighting seven-pounders in as many minutes. If I had to make a choice, I think I'd fish for Coho exclusively. They're fascinated by a strip of herring fluttering through shallow water on a single hook. They strike hard and make for an exciting play.

We stopped that night in Secret Cove and the next morning made Vancouver in three hours. No Tyee aboard, but each boat had a load of tasty Coho to distribute among friends.

A week or so later I compiled a resume of the trip. PUTZY had burned 237 gallons of gas and 58 quarts of oil on the trip to Rivers Inlet, worth about $100. The log book showed we had averaged 15 knots over the 600 miles, which, allowing for stops, means we probably cruised about 18. Cost per mile was 15 cents.

But hey, how much did this nine-day trip *really* cost? The short answer was about $75 per person. The long answer was substantially more, for Charlie had been more than generous with his credit card at all our stops for fuel and supplies.

OK . . . So I catch a Spring instead of a coho to bring home. Who's perfect?

How much more? Only Charlie's auditor knows for sure, for he's the one who eventually had to hide away some strange company expenditures for . . . fighting the mysterious potato weevil?

Far be it for me to inquire any further. Charlie had become a wonderful friend who company deserves many a free plug. Who's for next year?

52

Around Cape Horn Under Sail

Even 50 years ago when I knew Peter Thursby there were few men alive who had sailed around Cape Horn in a square-rigged windjammer.

Peter, then, must have been in his middle 60s. He was a small man but trim and nimble on his feet. His face was kindly although weather-beaten and he had close-cropped white hair and twinkling brown eyes. Fortunately the harsh outdoor life as a sailor had not gnarled his hands for he ended his days with agile fingers manipulating pen and paintbrush to remarkable effect as an artist at The Vancouver Province newspaper.

In those days I was newly-smitten by the spell of the sea and spent many happy hours quizzing the old sailor about those golden years of marine history. He had led a remarkably varied and full life before the mast until finally swallowing the anchor.

Peter did many illustrations for marine stories in the weekly magazine I produced for The Province and could identify each tiny penstroke of rigging and explain its use. I treasure several of his works which depict in absolute fidelity the myriad details of the sailing ships he knew so well.

Cape Horn lives in sea lore as the ultimate test for a ship rigged with square sails. These sails were efficient when sailing with the wind more or less astern (behind). But trying to sail towards the wind, even on a series of wide tacks (zigzags) slowed the square rigger to a crawl and sometimes even blew her backwards.

SHIP ~ 3 or more MASTS ~ ALL SQUARE-RIGGED

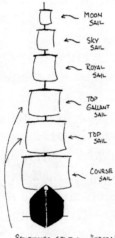

MOON SAIL

SKY SAIL

ROYAL SAIL

TOP GALLANT SAIL

TOP SAIL

COURSE SAIL

SOMETIMES SPLIT INTO "UPPER" AND "LOWER" SAILS FOR EASIER HANDLING WITH SMALL CREW.

Conditions around the Horn are such that a sailing vessel can positively whiz by going west to east but spend weeks trying to progress east to West, into the wind. These savage winds kick up monstrous seas which are compounded into a ferocious maelstrom as the powerful currents of the Pacific and Atlantic crash together.

The winds blow hard and continuously in those latitudes -- the formidable Roaring Forties, a wide band of westerlies which circle the earth. When squeezed through the narrow gap between Cape Horn (the southernmost tip of South America) and the Antarctic ice pack they pick up frightening speed and ferocity.

"No doubt about it," Peter often told me. "That is one rugged stretch of water--the meanest in the seven seas. We often sailed right around the world to avoid making that east-west passage.

"Running (sailing with the wind behind) you could make it in 48 hours, "Peter said. "But you would be in those boisterous Roaring Forties for several weeks before and after rounding the Horn which made for a long stretch of turbulent water.

"It was rough going either way. Huge seas would break continuously over the decks and the line-handling when a square rigger comes about (changes tack) is a real heart-breaker."

Peter learned of the sea the hard way, shipping around the Horn first in the 2500-ton four-masted barque Celtic Burn out of Liverpool. "Twenty

SQUARE SAIL   FOR-N-AFT SAIL   BRIG (BRIGANTINE)   BARQUE (BARQUENTINE)

dollars a month and all the weevils you could eat," he recalled with a wry grin. As an apprentice, only 14 years old, he was called on (like the cook and the cabin boy) to do a regular seaman's job. When heavy weather threatened, as it always did around Cape Horn, every man jack aboard was sent aloft to reef the huge flapping square sails -- claw them out of the air with bare hands and fold and tie them securely to the yards.

"The practise in British ships was to take in all light canvas at sundown," Peter said. "If it blew during the night we'd be called out -- regardless of the hour or our schedule of four hours on and four hours off duty -- to shorten what sail was left.

"It would take every hand aboard to tie reefs in those thrashing to'gallants (biggest of the square sails, hanging from yards half-way up the mast). The weather was often so bitter that we used to wear 'body and soul' lashings to keep our clothes from being whipped from our bodies."

These lashings were servings (wrappings of light twine) around the waist, wrists and ankles to keep the wind out. The sailors hated them because if they fell into the ocean, water would be trapped inside, hastening death.

Dangerous as it was swinging around on a yard 50 feet in the air on a dark, stormy night it was little better working on deck. "Handling the lee fore brace--the line used to swing the yard about when the ship tacked-- was the meanest job in the world, and especially off Cape Horn," Peter said. "The lee deck would be awash and as you hauled you never knew whether you were aboard or not."

With the ship rolling heavily in gales of wind, how does an apprentice carry a hot bowl of soup along open decks to the Captain's quarters without spilling a drop? Easy — you suspend the bowl in the centre of a large napkin which you hold by the four corners.

Cooking fires were extinguished during heavy weather for safety reasons so there was seldom a hot meal for exhausted sailors. Sometimes, on a particularly stormy night, a tot of rum was issued. By and large sailors ate poorly in those days. Fresh bread, vegetables and meat lasted only two or three weeks. After that it was hard tack (hard baked biscuits) salted pork and beef.

On the plus side there was a daily tot of lime juice to prevent scurvy--which is why British sailors came to be known around the world as "Lime Juicers" or "Limeys."

"The only pleasant day under sail was the occasional Sunday," Peter recalled. "British ships used to serve plum duff and treacle (a traditional steamed pudding). And if the weather was fine, we'd be issued with a cake of soap and allowed to do our washing."

But there was little real letup in shipboard routine. If there was nothing specific to do the crew was invariably set to the endless work of worming, parceling and serving. This job consisted of "dressing up" the standing rigging (the stuff that holds the masts in place, for example) by laying small line in the cracks of larger rope (worming), covering this with a bandage of canvas (parceling) and finally tying the job off neatly with whipping (serving).

Peter's first round-the-world voyage on the Celtic Burn took 18 months. After a spell in maritime school in New York, he rounded the Horn several more times as Mate in the Alden Bess, a general cargo barque out of Boston, and the Pythonomie which carried lumber between the Pacific Northwest and Liverpool.

These ships were good, hard-working windjammers but didn't offer the excitement of racing around Cape Horn like the illustrious tea clippers. One of the most famous of those racers was the Cutty Sark, named after the Scottish mini skirt which adorned the bare-breasted female figurehead at her prow. China tea was in great demand in England in the mid-1800s and high prices were paid for the first cargo to arrive each year.

Sailors relished those tea races. There was no hurry outbound from England and many captains sailed the longer but more comfortable route right around the world to avoid the hazardous east-west passage around Cape Horn. But once the tea was loaded every minute counted and it was full-sail for home on the shortest route--the boisterous but favorable west-east passage around the Horn.

Cutty Sark's first eight voyages were in the tea trade, racing home from China on passages of between 107 and 122 days. Later, in the Australian wool trade races, she reached even greater speeds. She completed one run home to England (in 1887) in a mere 69 days, passing other windjammers and even steamers with equal ease. On that passage she logged 365 miles in one day, an average of 15 miles-an-hour for 24 hours.

The Cutty Sark was a magnificent sight boiling along under a picturesque cloud of sail as many historic etchings attest. She lives on in stately preservation at Britain's Maritime Museum at Greenwich.

There was a huge amount of rigging on a square rigged ship. It is on record that the five-masted barque FRANCE ll needed 42 *miles* of wire rigging and 38 *miles* of Manila (fiber rope) to secure masts and yards and control sails. The U.S. clipper Great Republic probably set the most sail of any ship -- 15,600 square yards. Her mast measured 132 inches in circumference at the heel and soared 276 feet from the deck. One of her yards was 120 feet wide, twice the beam of the ship. The bowsprit was 62 feet long.

Manila rope (called line on a ship) is made from hemp plants grown in Manila and other tropical countries. It is spun into yarn, made into strands and "laid" (twisted counter-clockwise) into rope. Manila is subject to mildew and rot and heavy strains tend to "unlay" the rope and twist strands to the breaking point. To delay damage, ships often switched port and starboard lines on each voyage. In special situations they used left-handed rope (laid clockwise) which would adapt to different strains.

Nowadays sailors can use Nylon which is twice as strong as Manila , is elastic and will not rot or mildew. There is also polyethylene rope, made from a synthetic fiber that will float on the water.

Sails have changed too. At first they were woven of coarse hemp or flax and hung baggy and inefficient unless drenched with bucketfuls of water. Then flat-cut cotton appeared and made possible the taut sails that won the 1851 America Cup race for the U.S. challenger.

Today we have Nylon, Dacron and other synthetic materials which can be scientifically engineered to provide efficient propulsion. A sail, in essence, manipulates the wind to provide thrust for a boat in the same way that a wing creates lift for an airplane.

Modern design of sails, rigging and vessels allows performances un-dreamed of by old salts like my long-gone friend Peter Thursby. I won-der what his reaction would have been to that historic piece of film which captured Sir Francis Chichester of England sailing his yacht Gipsy Moth IV single-handed around the Horn in 1967. The weather, as usual, was ferocious as Chichester, down to a tiny storm jib, whistled by west to east through mountainous seas.

Downhearted? Hell no -- he enjoyed every minute snug and dry in a comfortable cabin, strapped in a specially-designed armchair in gimbals, toasting the many who had gone before with a glass of Champagne.

Now that's going around the Horn in style.

Captain Vancouver's ship Discovery
Painted by Peter Thursby

Steady As She Goes

Back around 1955 I spent a memorable 36 hours aboard the legendary deep-sea tug SUDBURY. We patrolled the classic yacht race from Victoria harbor out Juan de Fuca Strait and around the Swiftsure lightship on the open Pacific.

SUDBURY made her name through a remarkable series of adventures at sea in the face of incredibly difficult weather. For those trials she was admirably suited, having been built in 1941 as a "Flower Class" corvette for the Royal Canadian Navy.

My good friend Norm Hacking, marine editor of the Vancouver Province, was one of many west coasters who served in SUDBURY on North Atlantic wartime duties. When she was sold for scrap in 1966, his memories came flooding back.

"In 1943 we were westward bound from Northern Ireland to Newfoundland," he said, "and we ran into a monumental gale in which the entire convoy was hove to (drifting) for nearly a week.

"SUDBURY took an awful beating. The port wing of her bridge was carried away, her lifeboats and life rafts were swept overboard and a steel ready-use ammunition locker which was welded to the fore deck disappeared.

"The crew's quarters were flooded knee-deep and a giant sea swept through the galley, putting the stove and the cook out of commission for the last three weeks of the voyage. Those with any appetites subsisted on hard tack and tinned bully beef."

After the war, SUDBURY was converted to a powerful salvage tug (keeping her original triple-expansion steam engine) under Captain Harley Blagbourne of Island Tug and Barge Ltd. of Victoria and her hair-raising exploits made headlines around the world:

She steamed 2,000 miles out into the Pacific against storms that made other rescue tugs turn back to bring in the Greek freighter Andros Legend and crew of 38.

In 1959, returning from a towing job to Japan, she headed into 70-mile-an-hour gales to rescue a powerless U.S. aircraft carrier drifting 630 miles south of Midway Island.

In 1961 she beat through 150-mile-an-hour winds (Hurricane Hattie) to rescue a drifting oil rig, with crew aboard, in the Caribbean.

In 1963 she towed a 10,000-ton barge-load of salt from San Francisco to Vancouver in winds of up to 140-miles-an-hour.

Norm Hacking was also aboard SUDBURY when I made my one and only voyage and it was a supreme pleasure to be with someone so knowledgeable about that particular ship. I remember waking at night when we reached the Swiftsure lightship and thrilling to the seductive caress of the ocean swell as SUDBURY gently rose and fell in the open Pacific.

Too bad my old friend and neighbor in West Vancouver, Penn Taylor, was not aboard to share the nostalgia for he captained a similar ship in the Atlantic during WW2, as did his brother Jack Taylor.

CAPTAIN TAYLOR LEANS INTO A FORCE TEN PINK GIN.

Hacking first experienced rough seas early in life. As a lad he was aboard the Canadian-Australian liner AORANGI on her maiden voyage from Vancouver to Honolulu in 1925.

The ship ran into such a severe Pacific gale she was forced to heave to (drift) for days. A wave carried away part of her navigating bridge. Public rooms were awash, furniture was floating around and clusters of passengers huddled in prayer. One of the two engines broke down and passengers and crew were bruised by the uncontrolled plunging and rolling of the vessel. Hacking, like any normal youngster, thought it was all jolly good fun.

However, the North Atlantic has probably spawned the most deadly storms of any ocean. Many sailors and passengers have been killed or injured by immense seas and an alarming roster of large ships have disappeared completely. Force Eleven winds (60-70 knots on the Beaufort scale) have been frequent and can push seas up to 40 feet high, or more.

Maritime research in Britain has revealed that monstrous freak waves 90 feet high are not the hallucinations of frightened observers but can (and indeed have) literally torn a stout ship apart and killed all aboard.

Waves are created by wind, and records show this factor has been remarkably consistent for almost a century. But violent storms have been occurring much more often than in the past and oceanographers have come up with an interesting explanation.

Dangerous waves created by a hard blow often run many hundreds of miles in the form of heavy "swells" before dissipating their energy. If there is not a sufficient time interval between storms, these swells seem to piggyback on one another to periodically create a deadly freak wave which can rise 100 feet above the surface of the sea.

In difficult times you can always count on Captain Harry to spring to the rescue. Here I take the helm of the posh Norwegian freighter ANNA BAKKE.

Not to worry ! We're moored securely at the grain wharf in Vancouver. My good friend Captain John Fagerland has gone below to check the ullage before summoning us to one of his superlative banquets in the dining saloon.

Ullage? That's an ancient nautical word meaning what a cask or container wants of being full. Could it be that evaporation or leakage has lowered the liquid levels in our casks of port and brandy? Or that a conniving crew has surreptitiously siphoned off copious draughts in the dead of night? Is there enough left for this evening's festivities?

"I'll hold her steady, Captain John, while you check things out below. What was the course . . . 385?"

My wife Enid and Elma Wheatley relieve me on the bridge while I help Captain John find the missing hors-d'oeuvres and clap the scurvy culprits into irons. In the bilge -- of course.

62

Building
my Dreamboat

Plan A

One of the most pernicious effects of an attack by the boating bug is a psychological short-circuiting of the brain cells in that part of the skull which maintains a balance between dreams and reality.

The dreams of boat owners are simple and universal. Whatever craft you have now must be replaced *as soon as possible* with something larger. The reality is that it's damn hard to find the money.

However, dazzled by the hard cash I got from the fortuitous sale of PUTZY TOO which had become famous upon returning returning from Rivers Inlet, and with the boating bug fever running wild through my system, I was in no mood to think sensibly and boldly approached my bank manager with a rough sketch of what I had in mind. For simplicity I labeled it PLAN A.

The bank manager thought Plan A over for all of ten seconds and then, being both practical and humorous, created a rough outline on his blotter which he labeled

Plan B

This good-natured exchange led to a decision to adjourn for lunch to the local pub where we surprised each other by coming up with a compromise, which of course was promptly labeled

Plan C

The First Mate (my wife Enid) and I had long ago decided that what we wanted in our dream boat was a craft we could use in comfort whenever we wanted to; a boat that could sit outside year-round without benefit of boat house or restrictive covers, and with a minimum of bright work to demand constant attention.

The flying bridges and open cockpits so favored by summertime sailors were less than ideal for continuous use in the damp and chill that dominates British Columbia's coastal weather.

Technically our new boat would be a bridge-deck cruiser with all living space, except a small cockpit, enclosed. In the summer, large windows, doors and hatches would let the breeze blow unhindered. In winter an oil stove in the galley would keep the whole interior sweet and cozy.

In those days (the 1950s) Seattle naval architect Bill Garden was turning out some novel designs freely adapted from west-coast fish boats which typified what we had in mind so it seemed natural that our dreamboat evolve from traditional workboats which had proven comfort and staying power through thick and thin. And if she looked more like a utility vessel than a Chris-Craft, so be it.

We would call our new boat PUTZY, of course.

The day I met the Wicks brothers everything came together. Bill and Ernie had fished commercially in the open Pacific off the Queen Charlotte Islands. They knew what a workboat should have and how she should be built and they turned experience into sturdy trollers and gillnetters in a small yard on the Fraser River near Vancouver.

When I outlined what I had in mind the Wicks boys were skeptical. Then Bill brightened and said for "pleasure use" he'd streamline the foc'sle and wheelhouse and add a bit of fancy trim here and there.

"Change one line and the deal is off," I said. "I want her just like one of your log salvage boats — a large, rounded fish boat foc'sle, a stand-up tugboat wheelhouse about 6 x 9 feet and instead of the large open work deck I'm going to build an after cabin."

With these principles agreed on, I asked Bill for a set of drawings so I could design interior arrangements. He switched his cud of snoose from one cheek to the other and said, "Well, we haven't exactly got drawings. We did lay down some lines onct, based on Bill Garden's ideas, but then we got to changing things after we'd had the boats out fishing for a season. Nuthin' like a spell in the Charlottes to tell you whether you've got it right."

As he talked, he kicked aside some shavings on the floor to reveal faint lines of the original lofting. "We made up the first frames from these," he said, "but we've changed them some over the years. Now we set things up on the ways and move 'em around this way and that until she looks sweet. And there's your boat !"

Interior
Layout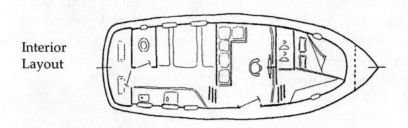

And so they did and I made many visits to admire their construction techniques — a mite more advanced than those I had used in building my first 16-footer in the basement.

Keel, keelson, clamps and 2x12 covering boards that could support an elephant were fir; steamed ribs on 16-in centres were oak; planking was red cedar dressed to one inch; and the stem, guardrail and bull rail were ironbark, that durable Australian eucalyptus which is so heavy it doesn't even float.

One week while I was away on a business trip the Wicks decided to give PUTZY a fancy transom and steamed the red cedar planking around such a tight radius that their handicraft was subsequently admired up and down the coast. And it gave PUTZY a remarkably easy motion in a following or quartering sea.

As the hull neared completion, I asked Ernie what sort of cruising speed I would get with a Chrysler Crown engine, the favorite of work and fish boats hereabouts. In reply, he fished a photo from a pile of papers in his office and handed it to me. It showed a sister ship to PUTZY throwing a huge wake and moving very fast.

"Boy, what have you got in there?"

"We've changed that engine now," Ernie said. "You can have it if you like."

"But what is it?"

"Hall-Scott," he said, with a twinkle in his eye. "Twelve hundred horse power. We got it out of an old Air-Sea Rescue boat and put in in the WIND just for laughs. Drove that boat 40 knots— but you go through 50 gallons of gas an hour!"

Needless to say I went with the Crown, a straight six that operated economically on 2.5 gallons an hour. My engine was brand new — still in its original packing case — although it had been build 15 years earlier during WW2. We hooked it up with a dry exhaust which ran upwards close to the mast and underwater keel coolers to provide a quiet and efficient system.

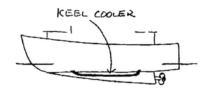

KEEL COOLER

As the summer approached PUTZY was the most unfinished boat I'd ever put into the water, and that's saying something. The Wicks had completed the hull and framed in the superstructure as per our original agreement and were pressing me for an early launch so they could put other work on the ways.

So I took some time off from work, roped in the ever-willing Pat and as many friends and relatives as I could press into service and introduced the 25-hour day.

We sloshed gallons of green wood preservative around inside the bare hull with mops, bolted in engine stringers for the new Crown and its 2.5:1 reduction gear, and drilled out the propeller shaft.

Bill, an artist with wood, took pity on my amateur efforts and cut some fine mahogany framing for the wheelhouse windows. Thank God! That job had bevels and miters and angles *on top* of angles, miters and bevels!

Ernie, an artist with blowtorch and boilerplate, made up galvanized water and fuel tanks, the dry exhaust system, and the chain-operated rudder and other ironwork including a huge Sampson post for the foredeck which was through-bolted to slabs of ironbark.

Pat wired up the engine, hanging the basic instruments artistically (and of course temporarily) from nails driven into the bulkhead. He soldered up the long copper keel coolers and attached then to the bottom of the hull, ran 110 wiring throughout for construction use afloat, adapted an old radio to the marine band for news and entertainment, and hammered, sawed and nailed like a maniac.

"Don't worry so much skipper," he'd say. "That sawdust in the bilges is only temporary."

I've often thought that the word "temporary" should be cast in bronze and mounted in a place of honor in PUTZY's wheelhouse.

From day one, problems arose which required quick, simple solutions so that work could continue apace.

"All right," I'd tell the shipwrights, "for the moment let's run that pipe through here. We can always change it later — it's only temporary!"

"Way to go, Skipper," chimed in Pat Tryon, my constant helper and Staff Captain. "I may have to re-arrange this wiring (plumbing, whatever) later, but it's fine for now" he'd sing out gleefully.

"Roger," I'd reply, banging galvanized nails hither and thither to provide hooks for gear which would later be stowed elsewhere. "What the hell . . . it's only temporary."

And so the T-word became a useful part of the ship's vocabulary. As the harsh winter days mellowed in warm spring sunshine and we got PUTZY afloat, it took on added meaning. Any improvisation was acceptable if it would enable us to slip out of the harbor and enjoy a spot of fishing or cruising or even just to down tools and yarn a-while with marine neighbors.

Boat building takes time. It's not so much the doing as the thinking, discussing and planning that precedes action that makes the difference. Temporary solutions often last forever.

Witness the magnificent old yacht CORSAIR 2 nearby, maintained for more than half a century by loving hands. Since day one a wooden whisky crate has served as a step when passing from the galley into the wheelhouse. The outside of the box is rich with varnish and a natty piece of lino is tacked on the top to link with the cabin decor. The inside has been turned into a mini-locker for those small items you always seem to need in a hurry — a tribute to that old river pilot Mark Twain who called it poor housekeeping to have three bibles and no corkscrew aboard.

Aboard PUTZY all hands knew that eventually many "temporary" jobs would have to be redone properly but who's counting when the years stretch endlessly into the future?

Alas, they didn't. After eight unbelievably short years I had to sell PUTZY and move east to perpetuate the family cash flow. Although I had lived aboard for a total of 756 days — just over two years! — there were hundreds of unfinished tasks, even to temporary standards.

But Fate was kind. The new owner turned out to be a professional carpenter who lived aboard and quickly finished things up properly and "permanently." Now that might have made a good plaque for the wheelhouse, too.

But I'm getting ahead of myself. We were still working non-stop to get PUTZY ready for launch.

Pat was a good mechanic — he had a restored MG in his garage to prove it — and often astounded me with practicality. When I mentioned that the crankcase breather was filling the boat with nauseous fumes he promptly vented it right back into the engine air intake.

The First Mate was a tremendous help in holding, passing, fetching, painting and making endless sandwiches and tea for the crew. She even found time to sew up a spiffy house flag in royal blue, buff and gray to match PUTZY's color scheme. Even Punch, our Corgi, got a bang out of the proceedings by regularly tripping the yard burglar alarm which set off a string of dynamite caps set in empty gasoline drums.

As launch time approached, PUTZY resembled a huge empty barn with holes sawn out of the superstructure cladding for windows. We walked around on loose boards over the ribs and floor timbers. The new head sat majestically in full view in the bare after cabin.

"I'll tack a couple of blankets around it (temporarily) to give the girls privacy," Pat said, "as soon as we get some tacks and some blankets."

The exterior, though, was in great shape. All the cabin tops (which were canvas-covered fir plywood) and decks (yellow cedar) were a sparking royal blue. Topsides and hull, all sanded, caulked and puttied, gleamed quietly in dove gray.

At the last minute I nailed a sheet of three-quarter-inch fir plywood across the engine-room beams so that we would have something to stand on while we steered. We used the big gas tanks as steps into the fore and aft cabins, which at that point were nothing more than "areas."

But the hull was sound, the engine worked, I'd spent all my money, so why not go to sea?

PUTZY turned out to be a wonderful sea boat although we had to add a ton of concrete and iron ballast and keel fins to dampen her high spirits. Total fuel capacity was 150 Imperial gallons. At eight knots she burned 1.5 gallons an hour, giving a range of 60 hours or 480 nautical miles.

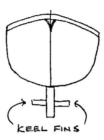

KEEL FINS

Gasoline at the fuel barges in Vancouver's Coal Harbor in 1958 was 30 cents a gallon, or 25 cents if you bought more than 100 gallons. One day when I had finished refueling, the attendant told me I had only taken on 91 gallons which would indicate the higher price. "But you're a good customer," he said, " I'll give you a break."

So he wrote out a bill for 100 gallons at the lower price — $25 — saving me $2.30 over the cost of 91 gallons at the higher price. Before I could say thanks, he said, "Look, I've charged you for 9 gallons you didn't get, so here's a cash rebate of $2.25."

I must pull in there more often!

That little windfall soon came in handy to correct a headache problem. The Mate and I arose one morning feeling unusually shaggy to discover while cleaning up the galley that those gin and sherry cocktails (like we used to make during the war when you couldn't get Vermouth) must have been a mixture of gin and rye! We had transferred a surplus of gin to an old sherry bottle for storage and didn't notice it in the twilight. Quick man, a better light in the galley.

In spite of our heroic efforts with formica, mahogany trim, seat cushions, lighting and curtains, the dinette was never really finished until the day our good friend Jane Beresford painted an Indian mural on the large bulkhead. As she worked she told us the brave story of Wasco the Sea Dog.

Once upon a time a native village far up the B.C. coast was suffering frightful starvation. Although the men were brave hunters and cunning fishermen there was nothing to be had except huge whales frolicking offshore far out of range.

One day Wasco, a local dog who also felt the need of a good meal, said to hell with just sitting around and forthwith swam out to sea, clamped a whale between his teeth and another under his tail, and brought them back to shore.

There was great joy in the village as bellies filled with food and Wasco was fondly scratched and belched over by one and all. All, except one wicked old witch who couldn't bear to see a mere dog living such a whale of a life and plotted dastardly revenge.

When next Wasco was far at sea catching food for the village, the vengeful old witch heated up some rocks and hurled them into the ocean. This, of course, precipitated a great storm which drowned our hero Wasco. And everyone starved unhappily ever after.

⚓   ⚓   ⚓

Queen Elizabeth was destined to play a significant role in the fortunes of my dream boat.

Shortly after the launch, PUTZY's official number arrived in the mail. It was to be carved into a main beam and inspected by the measurer before the ritual of registration was complete. This was paperwork at its best. Previous PUTZYs were licensed which was easy and free — fill out a form at the customs house and receive a number to be painted on the hull.

But I had heard rumors of sales tax advantages to be had for boats registered with Lloyds and interesting references to loading duty-free liquor. And I wanted a name on my dreamboat, not a number. I couldn't wait to apply for registration on the prescribed form.

It turned out there were several of them. I swore on one form that I was a British Subject; on another that I owed no money to the Queen and that she could borrow PUTZY any time the Royal Yacht broke down or the Royal Navy needed help. And the final form, so help me, certified that I had completed all the others! Cost: $15.

Incidentally, the registered tonnage (PUTZY was 11.3) had nothing to do with the weight, or displacement , of the vessel. It is a cubic calculation of enclosed space and dates back to the old days when it was important to know how much cargo, expressed in units of barrels ("tuns" of wine) could be carried.

And as for that cheap booze, well it turned out to be impracticable for small yachts. You *can* buy duty-free liquor for your boat at about one-quarter of the regular price but you have to go offshore (12 miles) to enjoy it. Inside territorial waters (Canada, the U.S. whatever) customs officials demand that the duty-free liquor locker be kept sealed. But then, as that millionaire sage Vanderbilt (?) once said, if you have to worry about the price of whisky you really can't afford to drink it.

Well, if you've got a boat you take your pals fishing. Right?

Do you ever catch anything? Hell No. But it's a ritual you ignore at your peril.

So it was that following some brash talk at the boss' Friday Night At Home Pissup that I found myself boarding PUTZY in the dark with fishing rods, coffee and the ugliest feeling in years. Two hours sleep isn't what it used to be. My companions contributed to the dark scene with dull fiery eyeballs and a skin tone akin to terminal jaundice.

They voted the water too rough to fish, which shows you the folly of giving the crew a vote, so I pressed on regardless. After a few minutes I dropped the hook in a likely spot, lit the anchor light and joined the boys below for a scotch and soda. At dawn (about three scotches later) we started fishing but in four hours could find nothing larger than a five-inch rock cod. Home, disgusted, at 1030 hours, knackered.   Jeez, it's not even noon yet.

During the early weeks of operation, PUTZY was plagued with generator (I think) problems. Her two new batteries were often so tired after resting all night they could hardly crank the engine. I felt there was something quite mysterious going on — a slow steady draining of juice when all those wires were just sitting around doing nothing. A fellow yacht clubber, an electrical engineer, said that was silly — there was no such thing as the malady I called "tired electrodes."

When I took the generator back to the dealer he said, "Hey boys, come and see a real antique!"

"Well it may be war surplus, but it's still brand new and it doesn't work."

"Looks burned out to me — but here's a replacement" he said.

That reminded me of a difference of opinion between Pat and Ernie when we first wired up the engine. Pat had said "are you sure that's not reversed?" And Ernie had said, "yes, I'm sure." But Pat didn't believe him, so they wired it up the other way. Or was it vice-versa?

Anyway, when I pointed out that the ammeter didn't work *whatever* way it was wired, they both gave me that pathetic look reserved for morons so I left them alone.

I have never understood generators, or the primitive ritual of "sparking" them to establish polarity, or whatever. Indeed, I became dubious about the entire electricity dogma in high school when I couldn't produce sparks by rubbing a cat's back with an ebony rod.

Consequently I felt rather smug when it turned out that the generator wasn't really to blame for our early problems but an "invisible high tension crack" in the distributor cap.

Aw shit ... I don't understand *that* either!

My summer holidays that year were due to start five weeks after we launched PUTZY. And who more fitting to have aboard for a *bon voyage* party than my long-suffering boss and business associates.

The crew had spent long nights and weekends aboard cleaning, building and plumbing to get ready for this first holiday afloat.

Pat and I wired up the batteries properly (permanently), built a double berth in the foc'sle, put in a dressing table (temporarily) and tacked up some richly-stained mahogany bulkheading in the after cabin. My wife's kitchen high stool sat near the helm and her roasting pan baster was ready in the bilge to suck up small leaks. The new white plastic galley sink and hand pump were installed but not yet connected to the water supply. Nipple shortage, which my neighbor Captain Taylor promised to rectify from his gash box. This is a navy term?

The ladies had been busy aboard too. There were tablecloths about and flowers and even mats on the as-yet bare floors (OK, decks) in the master stateroom and in the heads.

You do remember why sailors call it "the heads?" In the old days of sailing ships the toilet was located in "the heads" of a ship -- that portion of the bow which overhangs the water. A plank was removed and you stuck your arse out into the breeze and crapped into the bow wave. Running water and everything, and a chilling douche if the sea was rough.

However, none of that primitive stuff for our guests who came aboard at the West Vancouver Yacht Club promptly at the cocktail hour. After an introductory nip, we cast off for a picnic supper in Howe Sound. It was a warm, sunny afternoon but a lumpy sea called for a round or two of sedatives.

Soon we were tied to a large log boom in Snug Cove and broke out the martinis to encourage volunteers for swimming. It wasn't long before most of us were in the water (the martini mix was about 12:1) and Colin was pranksting around in his 1910 knee-length black swimsuit with red bands around the chest and skirt.

However, one shy young lady with luscious curves didn't get her bottom wet and so lost priority at the bar. She said that the bottom of her bottom was wet but the **ad hock** committee decided that the top of the bottom had to be wet too, although it was denied permission to make a detailed examination of the area of contention.

A superb supper of cold chicken and potato salad followed -- one of those gargantuan dishes that every hostess prepares in anticipation of **days** of cooking freedom. After an hour there wasn't a pinfeather left. We sat to dine at "temporary" facilities — the space where the dinette will eventually go was occupied by a bare piece of plywood loosely nailed to shaky supports, surrounded by aluminum lawn chairs.

However, with candles guttering (what else) in bottles and the wine flowing copiously, the mood was definitely upbeat. One guest laughed so heartily at the boss' sparkling conversation that she fell off her chair into the bilge.

The Royal Canadian Navy (do Canadians have hearts of maple instead of Royal Navy oak?) put on a free show after dinner, using the log boom to practice what we called "landings and takeoffs" in the air force.

Their cutter, which was really a longboat, I suppose, or maybe a pinnace, was a large lapstrake lifeboat affair with a short deck at either end and a boxed-in engine amidships. It was loaded to the gunnels with cadets taking turns at piloting.

The pinnace would approach the log boom (wharf) at a fair rate of knots, it's tiny engine thumping with pride. A hundred feet off a series of shrill toots from the commander's whistle would be answered immediately by the engineer (who sat about six inches away) and the engine would stop. Realizing he had undershot, the commander would blow a few more toots, the engine would resume full speed ahead and the pinnace would then ram the dock, all hands laying off the whistling and fending off to save the planking.

These centuries-old procedures seemed quite obsolete to our party. But I know Navy traditionalists like my neighbor Captain Taylor would never agree.

If modern electric or hydraulic controls failed, he'd say, you'd have to revert to mechanical linkage ; and if that broke down you'd have to use signal flags; and if you didn't have flags you'd have to pass hand signals; and if it was dark and you didn't have a lantern you'd have to use a whistle — so why not *start* there?

Everyone aboard PUTZY was in exceptional spirits as we cruised home slowly under a benign moon lapping up coffee and liquors. Well, you've got to do it right with the boss, eh?

When our guests had departed the First Mate and I had a midnight swim at dockside (say, those martinis have staying power) and collapsed into the new foc'sle bunk to dream of the holidays ahead.

As soon as word got out about the superb hospitality aboard PUTZY we were besieged by requests for invitations. Most we could safely postpone, but a few were special old friends we really wanted to entertain, like Kay and Stan.

This adventurous couple joined us up the coast at Egmont for a long weekend. I had discussed arrangements the week before on the radio telephone and as I was well aware that half the coast listens to these calls for amusement I tried to put the subject of liquor supplies across obliquely.

Stan, who thought it was just an ordinary phone call, finally said, "Stop beating around the bush — how much booze do you want me to bring?"

I gritted my teeth and said we'd better have about four bottles of rye, a couple of gin, the same of rum and some beer.

"Sure that'll be enough?" came back Stan's sarcastic voice over the air-waves.

"Well, that ought to hold us for Friday night," I said with all the non-chalance I could muster, "but if you want to get to drinking Saturday you'd better double up all around!"

As we signed off the air I could sense the laughter of thousands of invisible listeners. Stan and Kay didn't bring that much, of course, but almost. In fact, as they liked mixers, bottles came aboard in a profusion that would have gladdened the heart of Pat Tryon, the champion "for God's sake mix it with *something"* drinker.

The plan was to run up Agamemnon Channel to visit the majestic fairyland of Princess Louisa Inlet. Too often this mountain-rimmed beauty spot is roofed with rain and cloud but we were blessed with a day of deep azure skies dotted with soft white clouds.

 Along the way we slowed to fish lazily in the warm afternoon sunshine. Suddenly Stan's reel screamed like a tomcat. He grabbed his rod and for the next half-hour played the Old Man and the Sea. Some monster of the deep kept his sturdy rod bent double and brought rivers of sweat to his brow as he struggled for mastery. The rest of us were practically on our knees in awe of the intensity of this epic battle and waited breathlessly for the landing of such a prize catch.

After 21 furious minutes, by the clock, Stan reeled in a seven-inch trout. He was flabbergasted and maintained forever after that some absolute monster must have just disgorged the trout. Indeed in the photo I took the trout did look like it had been through a couple of ringers although we were never going to admit it.

Were we downhearted? Hell no, and starting the cocktail hour a mite early in celebration we carried on to catch slack water and slide swiftly through the narrow pass by Malibu Lodge into one of the world's most serene anchorages.

Massive granite cliffs laced with tiny waterfalls rose straight up from the placid jade-green waters. Then, around the final point, we came upon the thrilling waterfall near which floats and anchorage are maintained for all yachtsmen as a legacy from Thomas Hamilton, an American who reaped a fortune from inventing the variable pitch propeller for airplanes.

As the evening light faded and the barbecue quietly smoked up a mess of fresh salmon (caught by the Mate the day before) we made remarkable inroads in the weekend booze supply, considering there were only four of us. Four stomachs, however, well-tempered by years in the newspaper business. When I chided Stan for throwing an empty bottle overboard at bedtime he obligingly dove overboard, swam out and sank it properly. Didn't even bother to take off his clothes — my how he loved his rum.

Stan's behavior no doubt reflected family values. His mother was a diligent follower of the ponies. His brother, a streetcar motorman, married a French girl and was so broke after the reception in Stan's home that he had to spend his honeymoon there. Another brother was inordinately fond of the bottle and had, by some accounts, odd spells. Stan's patient father worked quietly in the Mayor's office for many years and must have had his hands full raising that family, for Stan himself, the poker-playing, rum-drinking news editor at The Province was not what you might call your average, well-adjusted citizen. But then, *nobody* in the newspaper business could be called average.

The next morning we were up early to catch our guests some fish to take home. And to ease the pain of sleeping on bare plywood -- the damn air mattress had deflated during the night as the Mate and I slept in the dinette. Shitty reward for giving up our master stateroom to friends.

Two aspirins, two cigarettes and two beers later your fearless Captain was under way for a nearby fishing hole. Along the way the others appeared and were soon lapping up a nourishing liquid breakfast.

Kay pulled in the first fish, a succulent five-pound red coho. When the tide hit low low we went ashore in a secluded cove and picked pails of oysters and clams. On the way back to Egmont, Stan caught a couple of small salmon and a huge ling cod and this all led to a huge fish barbecue on the wharf, spiced with bottles of leftover sauce. We rolled into bed early, full as wogs.

I awoke the next morning in the dark to find Stan and Kay dressed and moving gear ashore for the drive back to Vancouver.

"What the hell . . . it's only 4:30" I said.

"Jeez," said Stan, "my watch says 6:30 . . . I wondered why it was so damn dark!"

After some breakfast they left and Enid and I moved back into the foc'sle for a good "night's" sleep and didn't resurface until noon to discover that in the pre-dawn snafu Stan and Kay had left the substantial remains of the cod, salmon , oysters and clams on the dock.

What else could you do for old friends but run the leftovers down to Vancouver for them?

⚓   ⚓   ⚓

A month or so after that epic weekend with Stan and Kay my career path in the business world was abruptly derailed. It was really my own fault — in a moment of blinding insanity I told my immediate superior that he wasn't big enough to fire me, and of course he was.

My timing couldn't have been worse. Enid and I were poised to leave on a two-year assignment in England. We had sold our house, stored the furniture in Stan's basement, and the taxi to the airport was practically at the door.

What to do when Plan A aborts?

Plan B — "get out and find another job, and be damn careful not to challenge the boss on his own turf" -- was suggested by my pragmatic father.

Plan C — "life is an adventure," was suggested by my spirited wife. "Somebody's trying to tell us to go to Mexico for the winter and think things out. Chance of a lifetime. Footloose, jobless, houseless, childless and fancy free --why not!"

"And when we come back" I said, "we go to Plan D."

"And what's that?"

"We move aboard PUTZY and go fishing for fun and money."

And so we did, although as it turned out we spent more time cruising with yacht club friends than replenishing our bank account. A happy blend, though, for we sold a few salmon, shared many more with friends and unknowingly set ourselves up for two years of priceless adventuring up the B.C. coast. You bet, Plan D was a decided success.

We had left PUTZY in the capable hands of Pat during our Mexican safari and we were pleasantly surprised to come back eight months later and find that not only had he racked up considerable hours enjoying himself on the briny, but had also found time to complete many necessary improvements. Details were neatly entered in the ship's log:

WELCOME HOME !
Everything you see is, of course,
only temporary -- including the
sawdust in the bilge !

His handy work was impressive. A chart table hinged up against the bulkhead in the wheelhouse, covered with acetate for grease-pencil plotting. A small locker near the "engine room" held nuts, bolts and small tools. Topsides a yellow cedar mast and yardarm was complete with hoists for flags.

New mahogany-framed windows were everywhere, with real glass instead of masonite, and a new "permanent" wheelhouse door. An impressive instrument panel graced the wheelhouse with switches and warning lights which indicated modifications in the engine room below. And tastefully arrayed small oil lamps and wax-encrusted bottles testified to a bachelor's midnight entertainment of young ladies.

A brass-rimmed windup alarm-clock ticked away busily from a recessed mounting on the face of the new engine-parts locker.

"How did you choose that odd location for the ship's chronometer?"

"No better spot for it," said Pat. "You can see it from the bunk in the foc'sle, the helm in the wheelhouse, the dinette, and . . . by stretching your neck . . . even from the head."

And so we moved aboard to enjoy these welcome amenities, and to carefully stow left-over lumber, tiles, paint, molding, trim and tools so that PUTZY's face-lifting could be carried on apace while we fished and frolicked.

Upon returning to my yacht-club berth from refueling I found I was a bit rusty at boat handling and let the wind and tide carry me past my slip. With not too much concern I carried on down between the floats intending to turn in the open space immediately in front of the clubhouse. But the wind was playful and soon had PUTZY firmly wedged against the seawall with Pat's new mast and yardarm entangled in a laburnum tree.

The windows of the clubhouse, about four feet away, were solid with laughing faces as I fended off unsuccessfully with both feet. Amid a hail of hooting I had to leap ashore with a line and manhandle PUTZY off the wall and into her proper berth.

Although the Mate and I were serious about commercial fishing, PUTZY was not really rigged for it. So we planned to use our ordinary (heavy) trolling rods and reels, and strong nylon lines, rather than the normal trolling poles and power gurdies. Mostly because we had the former and not the latter.

We cleaned up the gear we had aboard, bought some new lures and one evening arrived at Egmont where the commercial fisherman were enjoying good catches. At dawn the next day we followed the locals out to the favored ground and set out our trolling rods.

I served the Mate tea and toast in bed and had just lathered up for a shave when a salmon grabbed my lure and took off like an express train.

We rubbed our hands in glee ... what a life! Half an hour and we've got a fish. Should have the boat filled by noon, and she'd hold about two ton, I reckoned. We carried on trolling for nine more hours but didn't hook another fish.

The afternoon sun was blistering hot on the mirror-like sea on the way back to Egmont. We poured a couple of long, cool drinks and debated the fate of our lovely, lonely fish lying fresh and clean in the hold. I felt embarrassed at the thought of visiting the fish dock to unload one salmon, but what the hell, we're licensed . . . let's see what happens.

I swung PUTZY alongside the fish wharf (an ice shed built on top of a large wooden scow) and tied her up. At least *that* was professionally executed. In a minute a young chap came along and I asked if he was the fish buyer. He said he was, and his name was Joe.

"Do you ever buy fish in ones and twos?"

"Sure," said Joe. "Lots of times."

With great relief I passed him, tenderly, our fish, lovingly cradled in a cardboard box on a bed of crumpled newspaper -- the Financial Post. Joe swished a bucket of sea water on the wooden decking of the scow beside the weigh-in scale, a large metal scoop that hung from the ceiling. He upended the cardboard box and callously dumped the fish onto the wet spot, eyeing it dispassionately.

"Coho," he said, and driving a pike into its head he flipped it onto the scale. "Ten pounds. Got a license?"

I produced the license and Joe went over to a small wooden desk nailed to the side of the ice house and got out his purchase book. He

83

filled in the date, name of the boat, license number and size and type of the fish. He glanced at a list of prices tacked on the wall and said, "Ten pounds of coho, three forty-two. I pay to the nearest nickel."

I gave the money to Enid, and the receipt for income tax purposes (!), and Joe pushed off the boat as I started the engine. Once away from the scow, Enid and I danced and hugged . . . what the hell . . . one fish, three dollars and forty cents. How simple can life be? We poured a round of drinks to celebrate although we well knew that we had spent more to catch that fish than we got for it.

"Obviously one swallow does not a commercial fisherman make," I philosophized. "Please pass me another swallow."

Two years after PUTZY was launched I was in touch with the Queen again. We signed a two-page Memorandum of Agreement complete with hereinbefors and hereinafters in which Her Majesty agreed to hire PUTZY "for the purpose of fishery patrol service" for the next six months, pay all the insurance and expenses and return PUTZY to me with one small caveat:

> *"...ordinary wear and tear, the Act of God, the Queen's enemies, Restraints of Princes, Rulers, and People, Fire and all and every other Dangers and Accidents of the Seas, Lakes, River and Navigation, of whatever Nature and Kind soever, during the said hiring, always excepted."*

For this the Queen agreed to pay six dollars a day, plus wages for the crew of $330 a month, a quite reasonable stipend then for an unemployed yachtsman. Well, you can bet I set my hand unto that document quickly. It was a ticket to Nirvana. The Queen, for God's sake, was going to pay me to go boating. For just a tad of work, as hereinafter described.

But I'm getting ahead of myself. The First Mate and I had no idea when we set out to follow the sign on the wharf at Gorge Harbor where we had put in to give the hull a fresh coat of dove gray paint that we were starting an adventure which would occupy us for the next two years.

The day had developed early into a cloudless scorcher and it was soon far too hot to paint in the open so we opted for a pleasant walk ashore through the cool evergreens.

In minutes we arrived at the home of Mrs. Robertson, sure enough surrounded by pastry masterpieces. She wrote occasionally for The Province newspaper and when she learned I was an alumnus nothing would do but that we have some coffee and visit a while.

Then she asked, "How do you like working on fishery patrol?"

Catching my puzzled look, she continued, "Well, that's a fisheries patrol boat you've got isn't it?"

I was mystified. What in hell is a fishery patrol boat?

Between slices of pie (it was baking day and there was a lot of tasting to do) Mrs. Robertson told me about fishery patrol boats and the people who were hired each season to operate them.

Nothing would do, of course, but that the Mate and I visit the federal fisheries office in Campbell River to check this out.

"It's true, all right," said fisheries officer Tim Cochrane as he inspected PUTZY, "but you're too late for a job in this area. Would you like to go up to Alert Bay?"

"Sure."

"On your way then. I'll tell the Inspector up there you're coming. He really needs some help."

We picked up new charts, caught the slack water in Seymour Narrows and anchored in Knox Bay at dusk. Nearby a large fish packer spent the night bathed in deck lights and noise as she took on board an unending stream of glistening salmon from a parade of small fish boats.

Next day, at Alert Bay, I walked along to the federal fisheries office which formed part of the Inspector's house and met Harry Granger who was in charge of area 12, a taciturn, soft-spoken man with graying hair and the infinite patience acquired on a job which entails much loneliness. Harry had been a WW2 bomber pilot so we had a common air force background on which to build a personal friendship.

With a lack of staff and the fishing season in full swing, Harry gave me a warm welcome and I was soon filling out forms and being sworn in as a temporary officer of the fisheries department with the powers of arrest and seizure "just in case."

"You'll be the local policeman and enforce the regulations," Harry explained, "but more important you'll help us keep track of the fish. Contact the packers and fish camps in your area and report overnight catch figures on our daily radio conference. Visit the main rivers in your area regularly to find out when and what arrives to spawn. On the basis of these figures we can regulate the fishing hours to make sure that there is sufficient escapement of the various species to perpetuate the runs."

Harry gave me a large portfolio which included a patrol officer's badge, an identity card, pencils, carbon paper, envelopes, diary and multitudinous forms to be completed (in triplicate) by the day, week and month to keep everybody happy.

I was to patrol an area of more than 400 square miles which included the top half (18 miles) of Johnstone Strait, Blackfish Sound and a maze of islands to the Northeast. Included were seven boundaries behind which commercial fishing was prohibited and seven rivers considered good spawning streams, although Harry said to check any water that looked promising.

At the time I signed up, commercial fishing had been open for several weeks and Harry was particularly worried about Robson Bight

"Anchor there just inside the signs, and stay there," he said. "I'm worried about poachers. We'll keep in touch by radio."

As I refueled PUTZY I reported all this to the Mate who was feeling rather left out of things. Although she was First Mate, wife, cook and companion, she wasn't on the payroll. Farther north and over in the Queen Charlotte Islands extra wages were paid for "deckhands." But the seas were rougher there and I knew she wouldn't like that.

And so, proudly flying the Royal Warrant (the blue ensign which identified   government vessels)   proudly from PUTZY's starboard spreader, we cruised out from Alert Bay to have a look around our new territory and find out who was doing what and where and how and when.

⚓   ⚓   ⚓

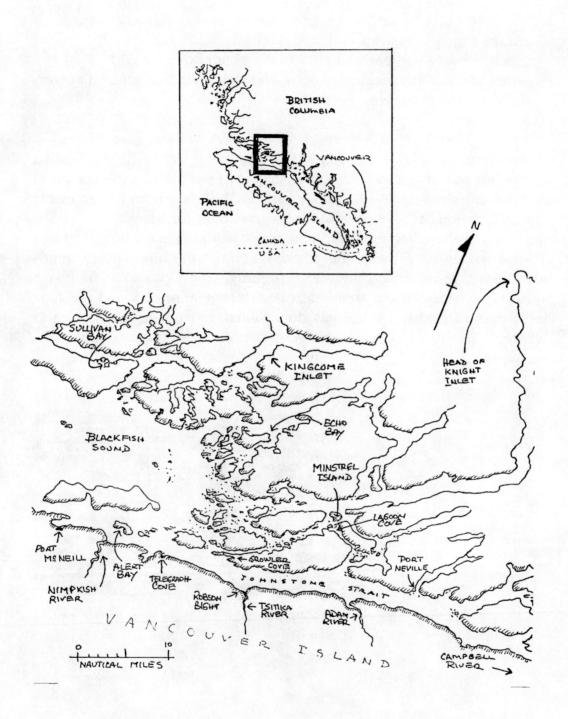

BRITISH COLUMBIA

VANCOUVER

PACIFIC OCEAN

VANCOUVER ISLAND

CANADA
USA

N

SULLIVAN BAY

KINGCOME INLET

HEAD OF KNIGHT INLET

BLACKFISH SOUND

ECHO BAY

MINSTREL ISLAND

LAGOON COVE

PORT McNEILL

ALERT BAY

GROWLER COVE

PORT NEVILLE

NIMPKISH RIVER

TELEGRAPH COVE

JOHNSTONE STRAIT

ROBSON BIGHT

TSITIKA RIVER

ADAM RIVER

VANCOUVER ISLAND

0   10
NAUTICAL MILES

CAMPBELL RIVER

88

Johnstone Strait , three miles wide and about 40 miles long, separates the B.C. mainland and Vancouver Island up at the north end of the Island. The mainland side of the Strait is a maze of islands and inlets which harbor logging camps, Indian villages, fishing camps and small communities.

The Island shoreline is fairly straight and uninteresting but is home to lumbering, fishing and mining communities like Telegraph Cove, Beaver Cove, Port McNeill and Port Hardy. There was no public road connecting them with the south in those days. Weekly supply freighters from Vancouver crisscrossed-crossed the area delivering goods. A lot of mail was carried by air and the service was surprisingly reliable.

A large portion of the annual salmon run coming down the Pacific coast passed through this narrow corridor. Fishing companies maintained strategic depots (originally canneries) where small fish boats could ice down their daily catch in scows or packers for the 20-hour run to the huge factories at Steveston, just south of Vancouver.

First stop for PUTZY was Robson Bight -- no ambiguity about Harry's sailing orders. This Bight is about 12 miles down Johnstone Strait from Alert Bay on the Vancouver Island side, roughly opposite Growler Cove where we stopped overnight several years ago en route to the sports fishing at Rivers Inlet in PUTZY TOO. (See earlier story).

The Bight is a shallow bay in a long, frequently rough piece of water. The shore dropped off steeply but we got the anchor down in about eight fathoms just inside the boundary sign. Not much shelter from the prevailing weather but a clear view of the restricted area and the mouth of the Tsitika river.

It was a glorious day and it seemed almost indecent to be accepting money for relaxing there in the sunshine, leisurely sampling a cool ale and whiling away the hours away like indolent millionaires.

There were more than 100 gillnet fishing boats and some 14 seiners in the vicinity but they generally stayed well clear of the Bight. Occasionally one would round the point a hundred yards from PUTZY, spot the blue ensign (or maybe it was the boundary sign!) and veer off. As Harry had predicted, just being there was nine-tenths of the job.

After dark a school of killer whales swept in, their harsh snorting reverberating off the rocky beach and scaring hell out of the Mate. One dorsal fin which must have stood five feet high cut by so close we could have touched it and a large watery eye gave us a suspicious lookover. I switched the engine on to remind them that PUTZY's keel wasn't a log on which to rasp off barnacles, although I didn't mention such thoughts to the Mate, especially after dark.

Made some coffee around midnight and decided to shoo away several fish boats tentatively drifting towards the restricted area boundaries clearly visible in the moonlight. They left quickly as PUTZY approached, lights flashing. Returning to our anchoring spot I committed a cardinal sin of seamanship -- I let the bitter end of my anchor rode slip overboard and of course with it went the main Danforth anchor and some 30 feet of chain. It was a new anchor line and I had been careless in not securing it properly to the boat. I put down a small "lunch hook" that held us for the rest of the night although a fisherman told me later that he usually just nosed into the kelp bed and tied a line around several of the larger plants!

A low tide in the morning revealed that all was not lost. The last few feet of the bitter end of my new green polypropylene anchor rode were floating nearby and so I could easily retrieve the rest.

The morning also revealed the 60-foot fishery vessel STUART POST anchored just off the mouth of the river where the killer whales rub themselves on the smooth underwater stones while digesting copious quantities of seals and salmon.

The POST had come in on radar during the early morning fog and had a large black bear skin stretched in the shrouds to dry. It had been shot by George, one of the fisheries officers, the day before at the Adam River some miles down the Strait. There were many keen hunters in the area. Knight Inlet was popular in the fall for grizzlies, and moose at a nearby inland lake. There were deer everywhere and no lack of hunters banging away in the woods at all hours.

I did quite a bit of shooting too, and went hunting with friendly fishermen for birds and game. I had three guns aboard Putzy -- a 12-gauge shotgun, a .22 for small game and a reconditioned WW2 Lee Enfield .303 "jungle carbine" -- short barrel and flash eliminator. The Queen provided shotgun shells for shooting sawbills (merganser ducks) which were decimating salmon fingerlings in spawning streams.

She also provided ammunition for the .303 so I could help the locals keep the seal population under control. There was a $10 bounty on seals in those days, paid when you turned in the nose.

Of course, you never have the right gun at the right time. One fall day George and I came across three fat grouse sitting one above the other in the lower branches of a tree. This was my chance to test that old theory that if you knock down the bottom one first, the others (higher in the tree) won't move.

But I had only the .303 with me, and missed with the first shot. In spite of the loud explosion none of the birds moved so I took more careful aim on the lowest one and knocked it out of the tree -- in fact, just plain blew it to pieces. The others still didn't move and I shot them easily in turn. Of course shooting birds with a .303 destroys everything except a few feathers.

"Hit them in the head," George kept saying.

"Well for Christ's sake what do you think I'm trying to do? Just wait 'till it's your turn to fill the pot."

The .303 was a recent addition to PUTZY's arsenal, ordered by the Mate so that she would be adequately protected when accompanying me on river patrols from the ferocious black bear and cunning cougar she imagined behind every tree. Although the gun had been cut down to "sporting" size it still weighed heavily, plus the extra 12-shot magazines which the Mate was sure we would need.

"Thirty-six shots to fight off a bear?"
"You never know," she said quietly.

I found it surprisingly pleasant to walk in the coastal forests. At the Tsitika, for instance, there was not much underbrush and it was quite park-like under the tall evergreen canopy. Yellow jackets and snakes (long, fat, green jobs) excepted.

It was harder going in the dense bush on other streams. When the woods suddenly fell silent and the hair on the back of my neck started prickling there was little doubt that a predator was concealed close by, watching with a calculating eye.

And let's not forget those bloody mosquitoes which attacked so ferociously that I had to abandon a couple of stream inspections and retreat to PUTZY. Great big, white, twin-engine missile-firing bastards the size of crows (well, y'know) and this in late September!

Their anti-social behavior would have interested a doctor friend of mine who after being attacked by seagulls wrote a story about "anal aggression" for the medical journal.

We enjoyed a great variety of bird life in our new area although the Mate didn't think it fair when four bald eagles ganged up to pick a squealing mink off the rocks at the edge of the water. We had seen eagles go after the awkward slow-flying blue heron, which was also unfair, but have also seen seagulls attack eagles and chase them out of sight, so who's king of the skies? There was a small colony of majestic golden eagles near Double Bay which seemed to be more civilized and mostly hunted fish coming through the pass.

Things became easier in some places when I got to know the areas. The loggers at one major stream were only too happy to take me five miles inland in a truck so I could have a pleasant down-hill walk back along the stream.

The Mate, who normally enjoys any walk, was not so keen on the woods. From the first she was disconcerted by large piles of fresh bear droppings and cougar tracks. When we suddenly came across a mutilated fish flopping on the bank she realized someone's lunch had been interrupted and looked around nervously at shoulder height.

"If you want to see that bear," I suggested, " try looking closer to the ground."

"I've seen lots of bears," she sniffed, "in the zoo in London. Great big buggahs standing eight feet high on their hind feet." And she emphatically rattled some pebbles in an old coffee can which along with lots of loud chatter and laughter warned all wildlife for miles around that she was on to them.

As for cougar, she finally spotted one while we were quietly approaching a remote beach one afternoon. "Look at that poor marmalade pussy cat over there on a log," she said. "Must be a stray."

⚓   ⚓   ⚓

The Inspector arrived by plane at Robson Bight just as I finished pounding out three neat copies of the weekly report on the old standard Underwood typewriter I kept in the wheelhouse. He was pleasantly surprised for usually he had to cope with atrocious hand-writing with those purple government pencils and greasy carbon paper. As he glanced over the pages his eye fell on a line to the effect that I had been cruising around "showing the flag."

"Jesus, Harry, don't put in stuff like that," he said. "You're working for the civil service now, not the Literary Review."

Then he mellowed and said, "When I told you to stay here I didn't mean every minute of the day and night. I want you to cover your whole area. Try and mix up your day and night patrols -- odd hours keep the fisherman guessing."

He asked me what I had seen up the river that day and I had to admit "nothing."

"I didn't expect you would," he said. "Cleaned out by illegal fishing years ago. But the Bight is a favorite spot for passing salmon to rest up. It only takes 20 minutes, you know, for a seiner to make a set and clean out four or five thousand fish."

I was surprised that seiners could be that efficient.

"They sure are," said Harry. "But they're honest, too. Out of the thousands of fishermen operating right now on the coast, only a few give us trouble. But keep your eyes open."

How true. A week later I made my first and only arrest in the two years I worked for Harry. And it was in Robson Bight, just as he feared.

I was awakened at 0600 by the Mate (who was on watch) to find two gillnetters fishing close in. I flashed on all lights and took my time breaking out the anchor, which prompted one of the boats to leave. Dawn was breaking when I pulled alongside the other boat and seeing he only had a few fish, gave him a chance to beat it, but he preferred to stay and argue even though I ran several hundred yards out and showed him the line.

He continued to be more interested in arguing than leaving so I told him he was under arrest for illegal fishing and read him his rights.

"Hell of a thing to do," he said. "I only got one fish -- there aren't any here."

I said everybody knew that and escorted him to the fish camp at Growler Cove where he unloaded 14 coho (142 pounds) and 8 chum (73 pounds). I wrote "seized" on the sales slip and ordered him to appear before the Alert Bay magistrate next morning. He said he'd expect no justice from that kangaroo court. I declined to argue further and proceeded to Alert Bay to report to the Inspector. More paperwork.

It was cold, blustery and pouring rain as we went to court the next day. The fisherman, whose licence number was 13, was fined $25 and $3 costs and his fish confiscated. The maximum possible fine was $1,000 plus a year in jail plus confiscation of all gear, boat etc. so he got off lightly.

After it was over Harry offered to drive the fisherman and me back to the wharf to avoid the heavy rain. But the fisherman was still arguing so heatedly that Harry stopped the car and told him to walk the rest of the way.

The size of the commercial salmon fishery in the early 1960s was an eye-opener. While you seldom saw large concentrations, there were almost 8,000 boats on the coast valued at $60 million -- 2500 trollers, 3500 gillnetters and 300 seiners. The balance were "combination boats" which could be rigged to fish different ways. Native Indians made up 17 percent of the total fishery and some 2300 of them owned and operated 1300 boats. In addition to the regular fishing regulations they were granted special permits to fish for food in the ocean and rivers.

Each of the three main groups of fishermen had different methods of operation and fished in different ways at different times and places. Although gear and boats have improved greatly in recent years, the basic techniques have changed little since my days on patrol.

The gillnet fisherman operates his boat single-handedly, works all night and sleeps all day. In 1960 he averaged $3500 for an 8-month season (with expenses taking 40 percent) and unemployment insurance green stamps to carry him through the winter.

The typical gillnetter then was a small, cramped double-ended boat, about 30 feet overall. A small foc'sle was used for sleeping and cooking. The wheelhouse was about the size of a telephone booth -- the fishermen said it kept them in place in rough weather. Many boats didn't even contain a head and the men used the time-honored cedar buckets or galvanized pails.

The most successful fishermen, the highliners, had bigger, newer gillnetters which were most comfortable and which no doubt accounted for their above-average catches. The boats sat low in the water and would run up to 36 feet. A good beam provided stability when fishing and a large wheelhouse/dinette made for comfortable living.

Gillnetters usually started up north and followed the huge schools of salmon southwards, fishing areas where the salmon rested or were conveniently bunched together by the configuration of the land. The fishermen had several nets of varying sizes so that they could adjust to the various species as the season progressed. The fishing company camps maintained large net floats where they could stretch out nets and repair holes, and stores where gear and staples were sold.

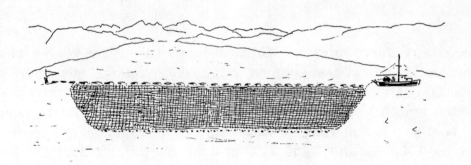

To set his net, the gillnetter first placed a small float in the water bearing a flag in the daytime or a white lantern at night, as well as his name and licence number. One end of the net was attached to this float and then the net was streamed out as the boat moved away. When properly set, a gillnet about 500 feet long hung in the water like a gigantic curtain, supported along the top by a row of cork (or wood or plastic) floats and weighted at the bottom by small lead sinkers.

With the net fully out, the fisherman drifted with wind and tide and maneuvered his boat to keep it taught and effective, fighting the currents which tried to twist it into a pretzel or wrap it around rocks and reefs.

On a good night (which to a gillnetter meant a southeast wind of 15 knots with lots of chop on the surface and no moon) the net was in the water about two hours at a time. As the fishermen bounced and drifted around in the cold darkness they chattered endlessly on the radio. Then the net was taken in over rollers at the stern and wound on a large power-driven drum. As it came aboard the fish were picked out of the net where they were trapped by the gills and sluiced into the hold without cleaning ... that was the work of the men at the camps who in my day got 1.5 cents for each fish "dressed."

So the gillnet fishermen sat out their solitary vigils. A bit of humor helped. "This is an average year for me," one fisherman told me as he cut away a large basking shark entangled in his net. The sharks have no "sonar" and frequently run into gillnets where they roll and thrash around tearing everything to pieces until beached, or shot, or both. "I usually catch two sharks a year," he said, "and one steamship."

Japanese, Chinese, Indians and Scandinavians, generally, seemed better able to cope with this monastic life than other Canadians. But at least fishing is an occupation of free choice; a man may gillnet, trawl, troll or seine, or turn to selling shoes if he wants to.

After lunch one day we cruised to Double Bay. As we rounded a group of islands, which seemed a good spot to do a bit of quiet trolling for dinner, we ran into 27 seiners. Boy, can I pick the hot spots!

The word "lurking" always comes to mind when I see a seiner. These large 60 to 100-footers spend a lot of time drifting around likely places for the seiner must first find his fish before trying to catch them. Aircraft are a great help when large schools of pinks, sockeye or chum are in shallow water near the shore.

In my day most seine boats had sonar and depth sounders to help locate salmon but the most valuable "fish finder" of all was (and still is) the eyeball of experience on the bridge which could read the signs of herring jumping and gulls feeding, and interpret barely-visible currents eddying around places where salmon were known to rest on their long journey down the coast.

Picking up a 1200-foot seine net is hard work and it was therefore not run out until the skipper felt it would be worth the effort. When fish were spotted, the seiner moved quietly near them and the net was run out in a half-circle and slowly closed around the fish, the tender pulling on one end and the seiner on the other.

As the net was closed, the purse line which runs along the bottom of the net was tightened which turned the net into a large bag. Slack portions of the net were then winched aboard by a big hydraulic power block on the boom and the bag reduced in size until the fish were trapped tight alongside the seiner where they were scooped up by a power-driven landing net called a brailer.

It took six or seven men to run a seiner, for in addition to a skipper and perhaps a mate and deckhands, you needed an engineer and a cook. Seine fishermen traditionally shared in the catch. Total fish sales (after fuel and food were deducted) were split into 11 shares. The company owning the boat (which may be the skipper and one or two pals) got four shares and the skipper and crew one share each.

On a good day an experienced seiner crew could catch many thousands of salmon -- so many that boats occasionally sank from overloading. If time permitted, seiners often hauled their catches down to Vancouver overnight for processing, or even sold them in American ports if they could get a better price.

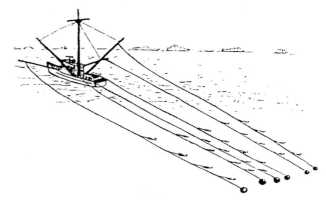

Up late to a dull, overcast day withspots of rain, to find trollers working near the island.

Trollers were the envy of the fishing fraternity. They worked during daylight, often had the wife or a deckhand aboard for help and companionship, and slept and ate at normal hours. With good gear and experience the troller was an effective fisherman.

He commanded top dollar for his catch because he delivered it cleaned, on ice (or flash frozen) all ready for the fresh fish market.

But there were drawbacks. A good trolling boat, especially for offshore work, could run 40 - 50 feet and was elaborate and expensive. A big diesel engine was required to drive the boat and the gear was complicated and costly which led to high operating expenses. In my day a lot of crushed ice was necessary to keep the catch in prime condition and supplies were often difficult to obtain.

The troller usually had six lines out, each with four hooks, positioned by four long outrigger poles. When offshore or in rough weather the troller could lower large metal stabilizers to steady the boat.

When fish struck they jangled little cowbells on the outriggers and the fisherman wound in the steel lines on a power gurdie (winch) to get the fish alongside where it was gaffed and brought aboard.

Trolling is by far the most successful way of catching tasty coho salmon and the big red and white springs. In an average year the troller will probably pick up four or five times as many coho as a gillnetter or seiner and twice as many spring salmon (chinooks). However, the troller ranks nowhere in the catch of sockeye, pinks and chums, the three species which because of their feeding habits are not overly attracted to lures.

There were more than 2500 trollers operating on the B.C. coast in 1960 with vessels and gear worth $30 million. Market value of coho and spring salmon caught was $6 million.

Heavy rain and rough water greeted us one Sunday afternoon as I returned to Robson Bight. Fishing was due to start at the usual time — 1800 hours — and seiners, gillnetters, collectors and packers large and small were turning up from all over.

An hour before the opening I had 20 large seiners in view. The fisheries vessel STUART POST steamed up and down to make sure nobody beat the gun. The smaller fisheries vessel BRAMA was nearby and patrolmen like me were positioned near the important boundaries in their areas. The Inspector was overhead in his plane watching everybody watching everybody else.

Promptly at 1800 hours the seiners, which had been cruising the shores all day searching for fish, ran their nets out. The late afternoon opening gave them barely time to make one good set before darkness sent them off to anchor for the night.

There were gillnetters around too. Although they didn't start fishing until dusk when their nets became invisible, there was competition to be on the water early to pick a good spot for the first set. They called this the "dark set" and it was often the most rewarding of the whole night.

Around 2300 hours the wind picked up and a nasty swell rolled me about dangerously in the ill-sheltered Bight. In another half-hour, rain squalls accompanying the storm began lashing down.

At midnight I broke out the anchor and got under way, and a black nasty night it was too with a vigorous chop and heavy rain blowing in long slanting lines across the beam of the searchlight as I cruised slowly around the Bight to make sure the area was clear. Then, clamping shut the wheelhouse window out of which I had been operating the hand-held searchlight (Pat had modified a war-surplus Aldus signal lamp which we used for aircraft control in the RCAF) I decided to cross Johnstone Strait to the shelter of Growler Cove.

This short run normally took half an hour but fishing was in full swing despite the wind and rain and it was my first experience in weaving through a sizeable fleet at night in poor weather and reduced visibility. Within that ten-mile stretch of Johnstone Strait, which is only three miles wide, there were more than 150 gillnetters plus the occasional large tug or steamer running up and down the main highway to the north. It took us three hours to cover the four miles.

Gillnetters, when fishing, usually turned off their red and green side-lights and kept a 360-degree white masthead light burning. They also had another bright white light at the stern so they could see to pick fish from their nets and perhaps other deck lights in the working area. On top of the cabin there was usually a spare lantern, lit in case it was needed in a hurry to replace the one 1200 feet away at the end of the net.

The airwaves were positively blue on a night such as this as the fishermen struggled to keep clear of each other, the rocks along the shore, and the not-always considerate commercial shipping.

Despite all hazards we made it safely across the Strait and along the shore towards the islands and reefs which guard the entrance to Growler Cove. By this time it was 0300 hours and the rain and seas were heavier than ever. There wasn't a glimmer of moonlight to help pick out those islands. Indeed, I only knew where the shore was because it didn't have any lights on it!

As I drifted around wondering how to locate the unfamiliar harbor, a small gillnetter with a weak light at its masthead putt-putted right across my bow, only yards off the beach. I turned PUTZY and followed closely, knowing that if he went aground I'd have time to back off. He didn't, of course — he probably knew that area better than I knew my own bed.

As we entered Growler Cove, lit up like a small city by the dozens of lights on the big fish camps and ice-filled packers waiting for the catch, I caught a glimpse of my benefactor's face peering anxiously out of the wheelhouse door. No doubt he found it disconcerting to have a patrol boat sticking like glue to his tail!

The big floating Canfisco camp in Growler Cove was a lively spot. It consisted of large 100-foot scows with sheds, office and store, and adjoining floats for mooring and net mending. A penthouse on the second floor of the main building provided comfortable living quarters for the manager and his wife.

I found a vacant berth and tied up at 0400 hours, made some hot chocolate and hit the sack for a couple of hours until I had to start the rounds and check on the catch figures for the night. Also made a note to buy a new searchlight -- one which I could operate from inside the wheelhouse and keep the windows shut against rain and cold.

We cruised to Alert Bay one day for a briefing on new fishing regulations. Harry, just back from a conference in Vancouver, was full of facts and figures. He said that a four-day fishing week the year before allowed 70 percent of the pink salmon run to be caught in spite of a two-week strike. For a similar escapement this year he said we would have to cut back to a two-day fishing week. We were then entering the critical period for pink runs and Harry needed accurate figures on fish in the rivers to regulate catch days. Fewer fishing days, he warned, might intensify illegal activity during the current closure.

An hour after leaving Alert Bay, I ran into the seiner QUALICUM fishing bold as brass in Upper Johnstone Strait. I called Harry on the radio and he said, "Oh, I forgot to tell you earlier — I've given that Indian a special permit to fish for food. But I'd like you to stay with him and make sure he doesn't take more than he should. Follow him around and when he's delivered the fish to the Indian villages, pick up his permit."

I didn't relish the idea of following people around unless there was some reason to be suspicious. But then I didn't have Harry's experience. He knew what *might* happen and was quite rightly more concerned with preventing offenses than prosecuting lawbreakers.

The afternoon was wearing on when the seiner completed its last set and headed off for Whitefish Passage and Blackfish Sound, PUTZY trailing along behind like a bad smell. Soon the sea began to pick up and the sturdy seiner gradually pulled away in the evening haze. By the time I cleared the passage the seiner had disappeared in a maze of islands.

I called Harry for suggestions and he said to check a small Indian village some miles away. After an hour of tricky navigation between the islands and rocks marked by patches of kelp I came on the village just as the seiner was leaving and heading down another channel.

At this point it was 2100 hours, the night was pitch black and I was lost in unfamiliar territory, so I anchored in a small bay wondering how Harry would take the news that I had abandoned the chase. I had begun to feel he might be right in his suspicions of this seiner and worried that at this very moment illegal sales were being made out there in the darkness. I began to feel that maybe you just couldn't trust an Indian, especially that mean-looking character on the bridge of the QUALICUM.

A half-hour later as PUTZY swung gently under her anchor light the QUALICUM steamed into the bay and came directly at me. Well, I thought, this is it. That guy's fighting mad because I've been dogging him and he's going to put an end to this "supervision" by a Paleface. Stories flooded my mind of patrolmen who have been beaten up, shot at and even killed, and I slipped below to load the jungle carbine.

The QUALICUM loomed menacingly large alongside PUTZY, her bulk dwarfing us in the darkness. With a powerful burst of her engine she killed way and lay throbbing not more than a foot off. As the deck lights snapped on I could see that large, powerful, mean-looking Indian on the bridge, staring malevolently at me. Then slowly he clambered down the ladder to my level and offered me a piece of paper.

"You need this permit," he said quietly. "I've brought it to you because you don't seem familiar with these waters and might have trouble finding my village in the dark."

At this point a small boy, about six, emerged from the galley of the seiner eating a huge sandwich.

"My son," said the Indian proudly in his soft voice. "We fished together, today, for three villages. I've just delivered the last of the fish and now he goes home to bed."

At this he lovingly patted the lad's tired head, climbed wearily up the ladder to his flying bridge and backed the seiner off gently so as not to touch PUTZY.

A gentleman, that Indian, and one I'm still embarrassed about following even though Harry was right more often than was wrong.

I checked Indian fishermen on many occasions, fishing from seiners like the QUALICUM or on shore netting fish in the steams under special permits, and found them uniformly concerned with conservation. They treated me well and became almost brotherly when they saw the mural of Wasco the Sea Dog in PUTZY's dinette. But they must have killed themselves laughing after the weekend I "guarded" the mouth of the Nimpkish River.

Harry sent me on this unfamiliar job to replace the regular man who was away on some family emergency and gave me elaborate instructions on how to get PUTZY past the sandbars to an anchorage a quarter of a mile upstream.

". . . to keep clear you line up the triangular boundary sign on the river with the fire-hall tower in Alert Bay . . . turn to port when you can see the quarry on Haddington Island . . . give the can buoy on the reef an extra wide berth because it's off base . . . "

What a way to navigate. I don't recall much of that sort of thing in the textbooks. But it got me in safely and there were jumping salmon as I anchored in the strong river current. Soon a large Indian seiner came in, anchored nearby and unloaded about 15 men who set out a net right across the river and started taking fish. I went over to talk to the skipper who said he had a special permit from Harry which was, along with some others, being held by the chief who was fishing in another location. Standard procedure — sounded OK to me and was confirmed by radio by the nearby STUART POST.

After a couple of hours the seiner pulled out with about 70 sockeye while some Indians ashore remained and took another 30 fish or so.

At noon the following day the regular patrolman returned and came aboard to tell me the Indians *didn't* have a permit to fish and had hoodwinked us all. Nor was Harry amused when he came aboard PUTZY later at Alert Bay for my report.

"Those damn Indians," he fumed. "They were *not* supposed to be fishing -- the permit was issued for the previous week but they held it over because of bad weather without telling me."

After a bit of palaver we conceded defeat by the Indians with a double gin and tonic. The Mate, who had been off walking around town with the bank manager's wife, returned to PUTZY at this point, which called for more gin to celebrate the capture of a *monster rat* which the First Mate had confronted aboard PUTZY a few days earlier.

Harry left in a mellow mood, saying that all us patrolmen will be more in the picture when special radio crystals arrive , giving us a private channel." And for God's sake watch those special permits!"

There was great variety in my life as a fishery patrol officer.

It was quite early on a sunny fall morning as we cruised quietly into Alert Bay on our weekly visit to buy fuel and groceries and turn in patrol reports to the Inspector.

"Is that chap waving at us?" asked the Mate as we passed the government wharf.

"Mounties seem real friendly today," I replied, waving back.

In reply the uniformed policeman on the wharf waved back even harder and motioned us in to the dock where the RCMP vessel was moored amidst several big seiners. We welcomed him aboard, poured some coffee and asked what was up.

"Good news and bad news," he said. "We've arrested the people who stole your whiskey, but not until they had drunk it all."

Now this was serious news up the coast in my days on fishery patrol. Liquor was hard to get. It had to be ordered (and prepaid) many days in advance and sent up from Vancouver on the weekly freighter.

"There were large orders of liquor on the freighter last week and the word must have got around quickly," he said. "Some Indians and other fishermen broke into the warehouse shed on the wharf that night and stole everything that hadn't been picked up. You're several days late getting here so they took your booze too — all except a bottle of Vermouth.

"Guess they didn't like martinis," said the Mate dryly.

"And now for the bad news," the Mountie continued. "Consignments of whiskey are insured by the shipping company but only for 24 hours after they are delivered to the warehouse on the wharf. You're past the deadline."

"You're a real bundle of joy this morning," I said. "Why don't we open a couple of beers -- the Inspector will be along shortly -- and hear the whole story."

So we did, although there was little more. The thieves had partied with the stolen booze on a nearby seiner and during the proceedings one of them lost part of a finger in the anchor winch gears. With this clue in hand, the police went along to the local hospital and found the culprit.

"You might say he fingered the others," said the policeman, opening another beer.

"He got off easy," I said. "The value of my booze was in double digits."

"For Christ's sake you two, lay off," said the Inspector. "Any more beer?"

I had the last laugh on those two friends at another party a month later. I had just received a letter from my insurance agent in Vancouver who said the stolen consignment of booze was covered under my "personal possessions" insurance policy and a cheque was enclosed. "The Royal is happy to reimburse you for this loss," he wrote, "but don't try it again!"

Beer was the favorite drink at most coastal communities in my day because unlike liquor it was readily available everywhere. You could stand on the one and only main street at Alert Bay and watch a thirsty patron emerge from his/her house at one end of town and be whisked to a waterfront pub at the other. Ye Gods, radio-controlled cabs even. Five of them in 1960 on an island with only two miles of road and no ferries to anywhere.

At tiny Minstrel Island — which long ago boasted the busiest dance hall on the coast — the pub at the head of the wharf had such a great turnover that they used an old flatbed truck to run cases of beer 100 yards straight up from the steamer. You could either drink it there or take cases home for emergencies.

There were even discreet deliveries after hours for regular patrons, alarmed by the local drinking water which had been tested and officially declared "unfit to drink; full of cougar hair."

Beer in those days came in long-necked bottles which would float upright in the salt chuck when empty. Concentrations of empties would gather in tide rips and we scooped them up with a fish net and soon had so many that we had to organize a secret cache ashore. Worth only 2 cents each, we easily earned $20 for Christmastime French champagne. But the crew of the STUART POST put us to shame. They arrived in Vancouver for an annual refit with 200 cases of empties to defray shore leave expenses.

Beer, however, was never a favored beverage aboard PUTZY. The Mate and I had become addicted early in life among the West Vancouver journalistic cognoscenti to the insidious martini and other invidious mixtures of the hard stuff. Indeed, a librarian friend was most disappointed I didn't title PUTZY's story "Pink Sheets and Dry Martinis."

Ordering liquor in advance worked best if you bought a case (12 bottles) each month, a month in advance, sometimes sharing with fellow devotees. The Bank of Montreal manager, for instance, where we bought the money orders to send to the liquor store, lived with his vivacious bride "over the store" where we were soon having lunch regularly and sharing our passion for the perky martini.

Weekends sometimes called for special evenings when we were welcomed with martinis, a hot bath and a roast beef dinner. Now *there's* a bank that really believes in customer satisfaction.

We had many good times together at Alert Bay and with mutual friends (The Wastells) at nearby Telegraph Cove, and I well remember that young lady's fondness of the old Dorothy Parker story: "I love a martini, or two. But after three I'm under the table, and after four I'm under the host."

Deciding *which* 12 bottles would make up our order called for a lot of compromise. But just look at those 1960 prices:

2	*Hudson Bay rye*	*8.40*
5	*Gilby gin*	*20.90*
3	*Noilly Prat vermouth*	*6.75*
1	*Peter Dawson scotch*	*5.10*
1	*Lamb's Navy rum*	*4.50*
		45.65
	Sales tax	*2.28*
		$ 47.93

Included in this bill was the Northland Navigation freight charge of $1.83 for the 37-pound box. One day we intercepted the freighter a couple of stops before Alert Bay. The Captain, a most genial Scotsman, found our order amongst the others and in spite of regulations brought it aboard Putzy. Naturally we urged him to stay and have a pannikin of his homeland's favorite tipple.

Now pannikin, there's a word I haven't thought of since I was a youth immersed in sea stories in Chums Annual. The buccaneer skippers on the Spanish Main used to reward their crews for dastardly deeds by singing out from the poop, "Well done lads ... and a pannikin of grog for all hands."

As I read those stories I imagined a pannikin as a shallow tin pie plate and wondered why sailors would choose to drink out of such an awkward vessel. It was years before I looked it up in the dictionary where to my astonishment I found that besides a small pie pan, it also meant a drinking mug of quite decent proportions. I'll have a double!

We spent many weekends at Telegraph Cove during our two years on fishery patrol and became life-long friends of Fred and Emma Wastell.

Enid, looking her sauciest in summer shorts and wind-blown hair, was standing on the foredeck with a line in her hand as PUTZY slowly approached the steamer wharf.

"Would it be all right if we tied up here for an hour or so to have some tea?" she asked the friendly, white-haired man on the wharf.

"Oh, so it's time to have a cup of tea is it," the man said, mimicking her strong English accent. "I say, that would be jolly nice." And then reverting to his normal speech, he said," Tie up right over here, my dear, and welcome to Telegraph Cove. As soon as you can, come up to the house where my wife is already setting out our own tea things."

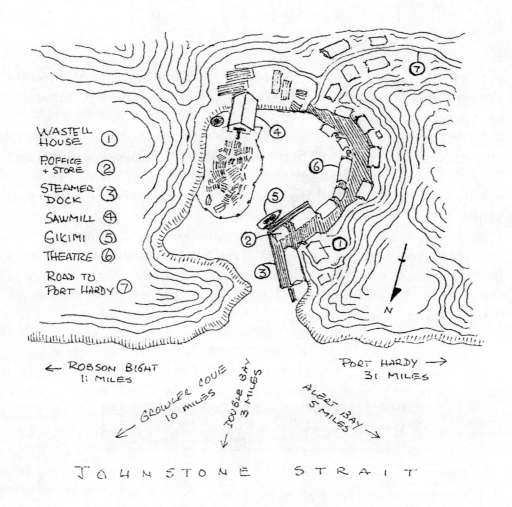

WASTELL HOUSE ①
P.OFFICE + STORE ②
STEAMER DOCK ③
SAWMILL ④
GIKIMI ⑤
THEATRE ⑥
ROAD TO PORT HARDY ⑦

← ROBSON BIGHT
11 MILES

GROWLER COVE
10 MILES

DOUBLE BAY
3 MILES

PORT HARDY →
31 MILES

ALERT BAY
5 MILES

N

J O H N S T O N E   S T R A I T

Fred was a gentleman of the old school with a tremendous sense of fun, an eye for the ladies and a vivacious wife who easily kept up with him. They had lived at the Cove since they were married in 1929, raised two charming daughters and kept the sawmill profitable enough to provide steady work for the 20 or so other families who lived in comfortable homes along the boardwalk above the water's edge.

Rocky cliffs rose steeply from the perimeter of this tiny bay, merging into heavily treed hills which rose ever higher to the mountains inland. The Cove had its own post office, store and freight sheds on the main wharf where the weekly steamer delivered mail and supplies, and access from the end of the boardwalk to gravel logging roads to Port McNeill and Port Hardy.

As the name implied, Telegraph Cove started as a station on the telephone/telegraph line which was strung along waterfront trees up-island from Campbell River to Port Hardy in 1911. There wasn't enough money to run an underwater cable over to Alert Bay, an important commercial fishing center, so a chap lived at Telegraph Cove and carried messages over and back by boat. Fred's father gave the Cove its name and bought up all the land around to establish a fish saltery. When that ended, Fred took over with his partner Alex MacDonald and established the sawmill.

When we discovered this delightful little waterfront settlement built on stilts that rose out of the water, an enjoyable community life was well established. Each Friday the freighter arrived with cans of film for a movie which was shown in the community hall as all the kids (and many adults) chewed on sunflower seeds and covered the floor with husks.

Afterwards the residents took turns putting on a late supper where everybody ate, drank and merrily discussed the latest events. Those were the days before television and lively conversation was cherished.

There were many features of our visits that especially appealed to Enid. Immediately on arrival she'd nip up to Fred's house and luxuriate in a hot bath and do her hair. I was close behind, for there was a constant supply of hot water. The fresh water line to these houses (which came from a nearby lake) ran through a copper coil in the kitchen oil stove, which fed into a storage tank, which re-circulated automatically when it cooled. As kitchen stoves were always on for heating and cooking, there was always lots of hot water.

Holidays, such as Thanksgiving, were extra-special occasions on which Fred and Emma hosted superb dinner parties for old friends. Emma had been a nurse in the Alert Bay hospital before her marriage, and Fred had grown up and later worked with his father there, so they knew everyone.

There were lots of new friends, too, like ourselves, and the young bank manager and his wife whom we had met earlier. And children, too, and grandparents, which included Fred's nonagenarian father who at the end of one particularly lively dinner party protested in a loud, strong voice that his brandy glass hadn't been filled like the others.

This venerable senior citizen, Albert, was for many years the magistrate in Alert Bay and during WW1 acted as recruiting officer. A young deckhand on the fisheries vessel from Nanaimo presented himself one day and was signed up for the Royal Naval Flying Corps. His name was Raymond Collishaw and he went on to become Canada's second-highest-scoring fighter pilot with 6l confirmed aerial victories. The fabled Billy Bishop, from Ontario, was tops with 73 and won the Victoria Cross. Collishaw spent his life in the Royal Air Force and won everything *but* the Victoria Cross. He retired with his wife Nita after WW2 to West Vancouver where they became our neighbors and good friends.

I recounted many of Ray's wartime exploits in the air, as well as those of Billy Bishop and other fighter pilots, including myself (different war) in an earlier book which I called "Memoirs One — The Flying Game." ISBN 1-55212-513-0.

Telegraph Cove played a role in WW2 when it was taken over by the RCAF and extra workers for the sawmill were brought in to produce spruce for building Mosquito bombers as well as guard the entrance to Johnstone Strait from the Japanese who were expected to invade after taking over Alaska.

The RCAF built and maintained two large airfields, one for seaplanes and one for landplanes, on the northern part of Vancouver Island during WW2.

If I know my RCAF, the "sawmill workers" they brought in to work at Telegraph Cove were probably all electricians; the experienced sawmill operators having been sent elsewhere to learn how to be mechanics.

"We were really squeezed for space," Fred recalled. "Most of the houses we had were still occupied by the wives and children of the men who had joined up and we certainly weren't going to throw them out. But by converting a room here and extending a house there we managed to fit everyone in. The hall where we have our movies was built as a combined kitchen, mess hall and barracks for the RCAF. As soon as we could find more space, wives and children of the servicemen arrived and we expanded our school."

The RCAF also took over Fred's workboat GIKUMI (Sun Chief) for use in connection with the sawmill as well as having a patrol boat of their own, with all the attendant security and regulations.

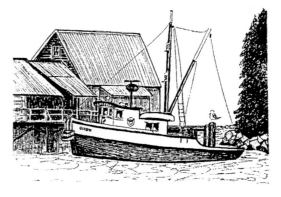

"You needed a permit to go to Alert Bay," Fred said. "You couldn't use the phone without being monitored. But it wasn't a bad life and we did contribute to the war effort. At least they didn't fix up the GIKUMI with deck-launch torpedoes like some of the local seiners!"

Throughout the years the small store on the wharf proved a wonderful way to reduce household expenses. All the groceries for young voracious families could be ordered up wholesale and sold at cost. In those days of mail order catalogues you could also buy, on the store's account, whatever your family required in the way of clothes, furniture, books, toys, radios, whatever, and save the usual 100 percent retail markup, or more.

Things were changing rapidly at Telegraph Cove when we were there. Fred's partner, who ran the sawmill, retired and a young newly-married Dane, Eric Vinderskow, took over. Fred was in his late sixties and also looking for help to run the business and pressed me to come in, but Enid who had lived in big cities all her life didn't much like the idea of moving to such a remote spot.

Apart from my business and accounting knowledge, the thing that appealed to me most about Fred's offer was the chance to operate the 60-foot GIKUMI. This comfortable tug /freighter/ferry with no-nonsense lines had been built in an Alert Bay shipyard and was so husky that when a car drove off a wharf there and landed on the after deck, only the car was damaged.

Fred and his engineer Jimmy used the GIKUMI to tow in raw logs for the sawmill and deliver dimension lumber and timbers to customers. She was heavily used to visit shops and businesses in Alert Bay and other coastal communities and ran friends, workers and cargo to Vancouver and Victoria.

And besides pleasure cruises for family and friends in neighboring waters, Fred used the Gikumi to take pilots on and off the ocean-going ships which docked in the area to load copper ore and lumber.

Much of this work, and even the running around on mill business, had to be done regardless of weather or time of day. Considering that the year-round climate at Telegraph Cove was preponderantly cold and rainy and the seas often stormy, Enid and I decided that our future perhaps lay elsewhere. PUTZY's logbook regularly documented both these features in unpleasant detail and offered vivid proof of the filthy conditions that more than once prevented us from spending a relaxed weekend at Telegraph Cove.

One Friday, after traveling almost 40 miles through rough water and a nasty south-easter, we had to turn back less than a mile from our goal. At that point in Johnstone Strait two powerful tidal currents collide and if they are running strongly (big tide) against heavy winds and surface chop, the sea becomes a maelstrom of whirlpools and standing waves that have to be taken seriously by anybody in their right mind.

We tried tacking across this last mile — zigzagging to take the waves just off the bow — but PUTZY would have none of it. Things started crashing about below and she was rolling and bucking in a frightening way. There was so much spray flying about that Enid put on her life jacket and started unlashing the dinghy so we could abandon ship.

Reluctantly (but prudently) we turned back for shelter in Double Bay. We tied to a large net float there in reasonable shelter but it was still a miserable night. The gale blew in gusts to 50 knots and it rained so hard that we wondered how long the large wheelhouse windows could stand the pressure.

The next morning it was 34 F and there was frost on the decks.

"Guess the swimming season is just about over," I said.

"And the boating season, too," chimed in Enid. "No wonders the air is cold — just look at those snow-capped mountains." There was no denying it; the nip of fall had finally given away to the chill of winter.

While PUTZY's oil stove kept the after cabin and wheelhouse toasty, the foc'sle where we slept was like a refrigerator. I was never able to solve the problem of moving warm air sideways. Enid had sleeping bags draped around our bunk to keep out the drafts and the master stateroom resembled a padded cell. When ready for bed Enid looked like an arctic explorer as she crawled in wearing pajamas, socks, sweatshirt with hood up and drawstring tied, and snazzy woolen mittens. Ditto your hardy captain.

At Telegraph Cove on such a night Fred would have passed us a power line from the dock so we could run our electric heater for a spell. Unfortunately the power for the whole Cove, which came from a generator hooked up to an old Vivian diesel from an abandoned tug, was shut off at 11 p.m. but by that time we'd have been comfortably tucked in.

While we waited for the storm to abate, Enid decided to bake a cake in celebration of our wedding anniversary. When time was up she opened the oven door and then quickly closed it again. "Cake hasn't risen properly," she said. "Needs a bit more time." After another 15 minutes (no window in that oven door) she did the same thing, muttering "that's strange" and then 15 minutes later a heartfelt "Oh buggah, buggah!"

The damn stove, of course, had run out of oil just when the baking had reached the critical point, and had been slowly cooling while we waited for the cake to rise. Shouldn't have been too surprised at the outcome, thought, for it was our 13th wedding anniversary.

The fishery job brought patrolmen a lot of verbal abuse and occasional physical violence. One officer, John, naturally attracted roughnecks although he was the most peaceful of souls. When a gang of rowdies ran amuck in Alert Bay one night after the beer parlor closed and rampaged down the fisherman's wharf to vandalize boats they picked on him first. John fought them off, drawing blood on two men with a big screwdriver.

As soon as he had a chance he nipped below and loaded his 30-30 hunting rifle. "If they'd come back," he told me later, "I was going to fire a few rounds over the RCMP barracks (nearby) to call for help."

"Bit drastic," I suggested.

"No bloody way," he replied. "One patrolman I know tried to reason with some of these donkeys and he's no longer around."

"You mean he's dead?"

"Yes Sir. Dedder than a fuckin' mack'ral."

John was also unfortunate in arresting people. One day he brought in three gillnetters for illegal fishing. They all pleaded guilty in court and were fined, which pleased the Inspector. But one of the culprits was the son of a local Indian chief and that displeased all the rest of the town. (The chap I arrested was a union official and that outraged *everybody*.)

Like most loners, John was a queer duck. One dark and stormy night I answered his call for help in patrolling an area where poachers were prone to gather. Several days later he was cruising through my area and saw me fishing for dinner. "Better stop that," he ordered over the radio. "You're in a restricted area."

"Well it's *my* restricted area."

"Doesn't matter," he shot back, and steamed off for the horizon.

It's lucky John wasn't around on the last day of PUTZY's charter. It was late November, fishing was closed, and everybody had gone home. Enid, The First Mate, was delirious as she reeled in the biggest fish of her life — a 30-pound spring — about two miles inside John's main boundary.

I must say Enid is a champion reeler-inner. She brought in that fish briskly in her usual style, just cranking away steadily. Anyone else doing that would break the line or pull the hooks loose. "Get one into the boat for eating before you start getting sporty," she said pragmatically.

The wharves at Alert Bay attracted many rough characters and the beer parlors fueled much looting and vandalism. One midnight at the wharf I awoke to a burst of gunfire. Couldn't see exactly what was happening but loaded up the jungle carbine just in case. On another occasion a couple of shots whistled overhead at high noon as some jaundiced fisherman (?) tried to shoot the government ensign off PUTZY's cross trees.

On the other hand, I had only myself to blame for a load of angry abuse I suffered one night at a party of rowdy fishermen at Minstrel Island. Fueled with a full tank of spirits I jokingly announced that all us patrolmen had been issued with cannon balls linked together which were to be dropped over all nets (thus sinking them forever) which were set behind boundaries. Trollers used these "cannon balls" as weights to take their lines deep and they were a common item around fish camps.

On the other hand I had many Good Samaritan days. One morning while plugging around on patrol in really filthy weather, rough seas forced me in behind Broken Islands for shelter. There I found the patrolman from another area waving frantically from a deserted logging camp on the beach. Lee had been stranded there for three days with (yet again) engine problems and was fearful he would be cut off the payroll for dereliction of duties.

Although we had to buck a big tide and strong winds (tearing a couple of Lee's mooring cleats loose in the process) we towed him up to Minstrel Island and through the blowhole to a mechanic's home in Lagoon Cove. Then went back to Minstrel Island where John, another patrolman on unauthorized leave, persuaded the storekeeper to open so we could buy Lee some engine parts.

It was late afternoon when we had done all this and we naturally repaired to the pub for a beer. A minute later the Inspector walked in.

"I was just flying by," he said blandly, "idly looking down from the Heavens and wondering what the hell all my patrolmen were doing so far from their own areas."

But Harry had a compassionate nature and accepted our explanations with good grace and a few beers. He and I were ex-Air force, and Jack and Lee were ex-Navy, so we billed the time off as Remembrance Day leave.

On another occasion I found two fish boats drifting around in the middle of a flat calm Johnstone Strait, the occupants too drunk to drive, or even talk, so out of compassion I towed them five miles to Alert Bay. The jolt of our little convoy landing at the fisherman's wharf woke one of them up. He waved at me nonchalantly out of his small wheelhouse window and said, "Send the bill to me at Klemtu." A bystander said Klemtu was a village upcoast on Swindle Island, but surely he was putting me on.

I hope that guy made it. A few nights later the radio reported that the wind had gusted to 90 knots there and blown the wharf down!

The fishery patrol job was the good life too, especially for an unemployed yachtsman. PUTZY with her rounded stern and heavy ballast behaved beautifully in bad weather, although I found it disconcerting from time to time to see the Mate, lifejacket on and a ghastly "abandon ship" smile on her face, standing in the cockpit with a butcher knife to launch the lifeboat (dinghy).

In good weather, though, she had it made. With the wheelhouse closed off she could sleep on peacefully in the foc'sle while I visited packers and fish camps to collect early morning catch figures or made late night inspections of restricted areas.

We found several pleasant swimming holes, shallow bays where the water was quickly heated by hot sands as the tide came in. No need for swimsuits although the Mate admitted to feeling shy when the local seals poked a friendly but inquisitive nose out of the water to observe our splashings.

We had a lot of time off duty and liked nothing more than to explore around the area. We were most content spending nights in the peaceful solitude of remote bays and inlets. One of our favorite hideaways was tiny Burial Cove which was indeed as quiet as the grave. We'd turn the radio off so as not to be disturbed by emergency calls, poke around the abandoned farm ashore, have a few drinks and with PUTZY drifting silently back and forth at anchor under the stars knock off 12 solid hours of deep, refreshing sleep.

A number of small farms had once prospered in such remote places and we found abandoned fruit trees still producing apples and plums and large patches of wild blackberries. One man still farming at Port Neville ran a small store where we bought free-range eggs, veggies in season and occasional home-baked goods.

We were tied up at the government wharf there one day when Enid decided to cook up some blackberry jam. No sooner was the pot bubbling merrily on the stove when a heavy troller coming in to the wharf misjudged his approach and rammed us hard amidships. PUTZY's rugged construction bounced the troller off but the severe jolt knocked over the pot of jam, spilling it all over the stove, galley counter and deck. In sympathy, the dinette table on which the sterilized jars awaited filling, collapsed.

A minute later a young boy came aboard to see if we were all right.

"Who's the bloody idiot that rammed us?" I asked.

"My father," said the lad. "He's real sorry -- the clutch broke just when he tried to go into reverse. Hey, let me help clean up that mess."

During the summer months we met a number of yachtsmen cruising the coast, and realized that quite a few of them had ventured farther from home than their abilities or knowledge dictated. I mean, what do you say when a guy pulls alongside in a two-hundred-thousand-dollar cruiser and asks "which way to Alaska?"

One day at Port Neville a tricky wind and tide caused me to make three passes before tying up at the big mid-stream net float. No sooner was I secure than a flashy American yacht arrived and encountered even more trouble so the Mate and I went over to give him a hand.

For some reason many yachtsmen find it strange that "commercial" sailors seldom offer to take a line and help them tie up. Sometimes they'll even wait, a few yards off the wharf, tooting their horn and demanding assistance. The fact is that most professionals -- and here I certainly include myself -- feel that "yachtees" should spend a few hours learning how to handle their boats instead of rushing around in circles shouting for help in simple maneuvers. Except at yacht clubs there often isn't an extra hand available when you need one so practice really pays off.

Running PUTZY daily for long stretches called for regular maintenance and I spent endless hours in the engine room cleaning or changing plugs and points, changing oil and filling grease cups. The galley oil stove -- our central heating plant -- had to be continually cleared of soot and the flow valve cleaned. I took the toilet apart about once a month to clean out stringy seaweed that fouled the pump and rubber flap valves. And of course regular ship cleaning, repairing and painting was continuous but tremendously satisfying to anyone crazy enough (like me) to love living aboard.

One highlight of our social life during fishery patrol was the visit of my favorite American, Cousin John, and his wife Virginia. They lived near Los Angeles where John had worked his way up to vice-president of a multi-national engineering company. We had visited them frequently down south on winter holidays and welcomed the chance to show our adventurous cousins some of the B.C. coast, and had arranged to pick them up at Kelsey Bay at the lower end of Johnstone Strait.

As if to welcome their arrival, the Strait produced one of its nastier days. Nasty? It was blowing like a bastard as we plugged south for the pickup. The water, beset by heavy winds and fierce tidal currents, was kicking up every which way in menacing whitecaps. They marched across the horizon like an approaching fleet of fish boats.

Five miles short of Kelsey Bay a hard driving rain cut visibility to zero and a boisterous south-easter lashed the Strait into long ridges of foaming whitecaps. PUTZY rolled heavily as we quartered the seas and threw such hefty clouds of spray over the wheelhouse that the windshield wipers couldn't keep up. We were taking solid green ones over the stemhead, I could hear things crashing around below and then I caught a glimpse of the First Mate, white-faced in the cockpit tying on her lifejacket.

There was just no way we were going to make Kelsey Bay that day, so I turned back and retreated to shelter in a small cove.

"Why didn't you put on your lifejacket?" The Mate asked as she came into the wheelhouse as we tied up to the wharf.

"No time. If I'd let go of the wheel I think I'd have fallen down."

"Well this will straighten you up," she said, producing a large glass of strait Scotch. Her hand was shaking so violently that some of the liquor splashed out before I could get the glass to my lips. Or was it *my* hand that was shaking? It had been the roughest ride we ever experienced in PUTZY.

"No wonder you get to love boats," I said. "The Wicks told me that PUTZY would still be crashing along when everyone aboard had died of fright."

"I just about did," confessed the Mate. "Let's have another drink."

I got Cousin John on the radio and said we would try again next morning. This wasn't a good idea, for the seas were even worse than before, forcing me to turn back once again. Realizing our predicament, Cousin John chartered a small float plane and whizzed by us in the Strait, motioning us into a nearby sheltered cove. Half an hour later he was pouring us all stiff "shooters" from his traveling flask of bourbon and the holiday cruise was finally on.

John and Virginia enjoyed themselves hugely as we spent a week doing our regular patrol jobs and then a few more days on leave fishing, sightseeing and loafing. John was continually amazed at the machinery and equipment rusting away at abandoned logging sites. "These old cables, miles of them, just lying here," he said. Worth a bloody fortune in Los Angeles."

"Well why don't you barge a load of them out and sell them?"

"Yeah, that's possible. The costs would be high but I'm sure going to check them out as soon as I get back."

Which he undoubtedly did through his big engineering firm there, but we never heard anything more on the subject.

Virginia celebrated her birthday while the Cousins were aboard and I served a breakfast special to all hands while they were still in bed.

> *Stir gently in a glass:*
> *1 egg*
> *1 lump sugar*
> *8 oz fruit juice*
> *3 oz rum*
> ***Guaranteed to produce hearty cries for "seconds."***

⚓   ⚓   ⚓

The Mate and I enjoyed a lot of good fishing, for pleasure and for the pot. There were always tasty cutthroat or dolly varden trout to be had around the mouths of my rivers, as well as steelhead up the Adam or Kokish, and cod, red snapper and five varieties of salmon in the ocean, although we didn't care for dog salmon.

"Please don't call them "dogs" in your reports," Harry said. "I know the fishermen do, but headquarters would rather you use the proper name — chum salmon."

I had a hard time remembering this correct name until the mate said, "Don't forget, a dog is a fisherman's best chum."

There were many other edibles to hand in the sea, and we ate almost everything except the Japanese favorites, the spiney sea urchin and the hard-to-gather and hard-to-prepare abalone. The log-book was full of revealing entries:

> *"... filled a pail with ice at the B.C. Packers*
> *scow in Growler to keep those lovely trout*
> *fresh until we can eat them. That's after we*
> *eat the steak, also on ice..."*

We stuffed ourselves regularly on clams and crabs. The clams, we learned, would self-clean all the grit out of their systems if left in a pail of sea water which had been enriched with oatmeal.

Crabs were everywhere — frisky Dungeness monsters that would barely fit into a galvanized pail of boiling water. And what price toasted crab sandwiches at midnight on anchor watch while the wind howled and the rain hammered down.

For a special treat Enid would pry big black mussels off rocks or old pilings, dress them up with a white wine sauce and serve them as that French delicacy *moules marinière*. Mind, we had to substitute Vermouth for the white wine, but that's roughing it for you.

And of course there were the almost-daily inspection of rivers and streams in which you could usually find a tasty trout or two, and occasionally a fall steelhead.

Incidentally, we quickly learned not to keep old fish heads (for the crab net) in the cockpit overnight. Marauding raccoons and otter plagued most wharves and floats.

More than once we awoke to an unholy racket as the lively little otters thumped around on top of the float and then dove underneath to gnaw away noisily on barnacles and mussels. Crows were usually fascinated by this activity and would caw and peck the wharf in approval. Seagulls would joined in too and drop clams on the wharf (or PUTZY) from a great height to break open for easy consumption.

The fishermen were constantly sharing choice edibles. Steelhead, occasionally caught in gillnets, were supremely tasty when grilled or barbecued with a bit of bacon.

One afternoon we were tied up at Bones Bay (hot showers always available to friends of the management) when the 46-foot troller SAILOR LAD of Egmont came in. We knew these boys well — they had built their skookum boat themselves and spent time trolling and packing fish to the market.

This day they were trying something different, and were cooking up a large catch of jumbo prawns on a steaming cauldron on the after deck. I went over with a saucepan to buy a few.

"What the hell," said the skipper. "Haven't you got a bucket?"

"Sure, but I can't afford that many."

"So who's talking about paying?"

"Well how are you going to make a living?"

"We've got enough to feed half of Vancouver. There's big prawn beds here but we haven't yet figured out how to get 'em to market quick and regular."

And I don't think they ever did. I was surprised the big fishing companies which had all the necessary facilities didn't have a go. Maybe they did and like SAILOR LAD found it just wasn't feasible without costly air transport to big U.S. markets.

When we tired of seafood there was that fabulous butcher at Minstrel Island. I was watching him cut up a side of beef the steamer had just brought in and noticed that he was slicing off some small tasty morsels and dropping them in a box, like scraps.

124

"Why are you keeping those crappy old bits, Joe?"

He gave me a hard look and didn't reply.

"I'll give you a dollar a pound for them," I said.

"Waall," he hesitated some more, knowing they weren't really scraps and realizing that I also knew they weren't scraps. "Waall OK, but don't tell anybody."

What Joe was doing was cutting up a side of beef into steaks for a logging camp in the area. "Those guys only want one thing in a steak and that's size," he explained. "As long as it's bigger than the plate, it's good. So I cut the meat that way to suit them, and trim off the little filets for guys like you and me who prefer quality instead of quantity."

Joe could usually supply PUTZY with six of the choice little filet mignons each week, plus bacon to wrap around the edges. At a dollar a pound, these three dinners cost us a mere $1.50 and the Queen usually paid. Joe the butcher, you see, was also Joe the wharfinger and ran the gas dock where I refueled PUTZY each week. The Queen paid for PUTZY's fuel, grease and oil with warrants and Joe continually got the gas and grocery orders confused and put them all on her bill. I spoke severely to him about this but he never paid any attention. Now there's one hell of a butcher for you.

Like all good things, this idyllic spell of yachting around on the Queen's expense account had to come to an end. Before I knew it two years had passed. The weather was unusually rough and cold that fall and although PUTZY was cheerful and toasty inside, there was snow on the decks which prompted the Mate to launch a vigorous campaign for a long shore leave. Like forever.

The log book provided her with a good argument. In 1960, our first year on the fisheries job, we had spent 230 days aboard PUTZY and patrolled 1660 miles out of our base at Alert Bay. It was the worst year for salmon catches since records started in 1910 and many fishermen spent weeks "fishing for stamps" — just drifting about collecting weekly stamps which determined the amount of unemployment insurance they would receive in the winter. The Vancouver Province newspaper reported that the catch was so poor that shoplifters in Britain, whose first choice was B.C. canned salmon, were complaining.

My good friend Bill Nayler who owned Ruxton Island told me he knew why the trollers, at least, didn't catch many fish. "They didn't make enough sandwiches."

"Oh, how does that work?"

"Well, when I was trolling for a living I soon learned that the warning bells (on the outriggers) would always start jangling the moment I went below to fix up something to eat."

Always?"

"Yeah, although sometimes I had to spend most of the day in the galley to bring on a lucky streak."

"Must have eaten a lot of sandwiches."

"I get bilious now just *thinking* of bread and jelly."

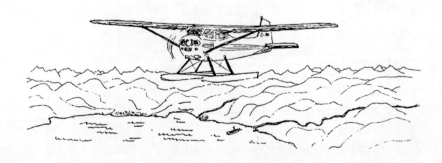

PUTZY's second year (1961) on patrol was quite different. We spent 215 days aboard and patrolled 3218 miles out of Minstrel Island, covering the surrounding waters and the lower end of Johnstone Strait.

That year was fantastic for fishermen, and conservation too. One August day at the Adam River, Harry and I (working from the ground and the air) estimated 25,000 pinks in the first five miles of the river. Plus a school of 10,000 more in the ocean at the river mouth waiting to enter.

The mouth of the Adam River is completely exposed to Johnstone Strait's notorious weather. Once when I complained about anchoring there when it was blowing, Harry said a previous patrolman used to go a few hundred yards upstream and anchor in a "hole" of deep water. There's a hole there all right, which is a good place to catch trout, but I couldn't see how I could get PUTZY in there without wheels.

In calm weather, however, the Adam River mouth was magnificent at night as the fish decorated the moonlit waters with brilliant flashes of sparkling phosphorescence as they zipped about close to the surface like miniature torpedoes, leaving dazzling trails of sparkling silvery bubbles.

Gillnetters in the area, when fishing was open, numbered between 500 and 600. One evening more than 90 seiners averaged 1,000 fish each. A lot of fishermen talked of earning $20,000 or more that season and it sounded quite reasonable. They were getting 32 cents a pound for sockeye then, 11 cents for pinks, 24 cents for coho, 13 cents for chums and 50 cents for big red springs (chinook).

Fishermen traditionally complain about the low level of prices, and with good reason. Old records from 1902, when Alert Bay Cannery had a monopoly on buying fish for miles around, reveal the going rate for sockeye was 7 cents *per fish.!*

It was late November when that second patrol ended and rough seas and stormy weather delayed our departure. Winds gusted to 65 knots one night and I had to double up the mooring lines to a large fish scow and even take the flag down. But at least I had some time to write Christmas cards.

As we left for home, gale warnings persisted and it was snowing. Four large snow geese wheeled overhead, giving the Mate a chance to expound on her favorite story about humming birds that tuck in under the huge wings of the geese for a free ride south.

It took us a week to return to Vancouver, and it was snowing again when I tied up at Bert Menchions shipyard. The First Mate hit the wharf running and didn't come back for two hours.

"What's up?" I asked.

"You're romance with the Queen is over," she announced. "I've found an apartment beside Stanley Park and we're moving ashore this afternoon. Two years up the coast has been fun, and I love you dearly, but I didn't marry a sailor. Now it's time to settle down in a proper job on shore. And I mean something *permanent !"*

We had four more years of weekend and holiday cruising aboard PUTZY before we put her up for sale, but it wasn't quite the same. I missed Harry, and Joe, and even those disgruntled fishermen who had taken the odd shot at me. Most of all I missed the relaxed holiday atmosphere of long spells aboard with the Queen picking up the tab.

After Alert Bay, local events like fish derbies were rather tame even though there were more bottles flying around than seagulls. None the less I didn't get much sleep at Gibsons Landing one night. Rowdy sports (?) fishermen roamed the wharves getting tanked up for the big fish derby which was to start at dawn. One returnee from the local pub tripped over his cockpit combing and had quite a swim before we fished him out and put him to bed. Another celebrant carelessly flipped a lighted cigarette butt onto a canvas cockpit cover. Owner of the boat, asleep below, didn't mind — he thought someone else's boat was on fire. The firebug got so excited over his work that he danced a jig right off the end of the wharf into the salt chuck.

We cruised weekends in Howe Sound with yacht club friends, fished around Pender Harbor, enjoyed the annual Saturna Island lamb barbecues and explored De Courcey Island for traces of Brother Xll's weird cult and visited Seattle to see the World's Fair. I ran PUTZY on a sandbar there and had to call the coast guard for assistance.

Well, that wasn't as embarrassing though as my arrival at the yacht club one day, hanging over the stern steering PUTZY with a piece of plywood decking I had ripped up below. The damn rudder had fallen off completely -- electrolysis -- which called for another expensive visit to Menchions shipyard.

I got to know Bert Menchions one winter at a Power Squadron course. We had been lectured on boat construction by a local marine architect and got to gossiping around the blackboard during intermission. Someone asked the difference between the keel and the keelson and with the false confidence gained during years of writing about boats I pointed to the diagrams on the board and identified them.

Then, from the back of the group came a quiet voice: "I think you've got them backwards."

"And who," I asked blustering with embarrassment, "are you?"

"I'm Bert Menchions," said the quiet little man. "I run a small shipyard in town."

He was dead right, of course, and I happily patronized his yard ever after.

During those years we took many friends and relatives for day and weekend cruises and one somber afternoon scattered the ashes of my dear old friend Laurence Johannson in the ocean near his waterfront home.

I went out cruising a few weekends by myself -- to enjoy some good cooking I facetiously told the First Mate. Sometimes Pat came along. Once when we were half-way across an extremely lumpy Strait of Georgia that panicky smell of fire swept through PUTZY.

Pat dashed below, ready to keep on going and abandon ship over the stern if the flames were anywhere near the gas tanks. But he skidded to an amazed stop when he noticed his socks, carefully draped over the warm (at anchor) exhaust stack to dry from a walk ashore earlier, were smoldering pungently.

"Quick man, a double gin to quench the stench!"

Cousin John from LA , a rather careful man with a dollar although he had many, came aboard for an afternoon cruise and grandly offered to pay for a few gallons of gas. I just couldn't resist filling the tanks to the brim on his credit card — 140 gallons!

Perhaps the best laugh we enjoyed came from our 10-year-old nephew Roddy. This lad had slept overnight in the cockpit under the stars and reported the next morning in all seriousness that the heavens "looked just like the Vancouver planetarium."

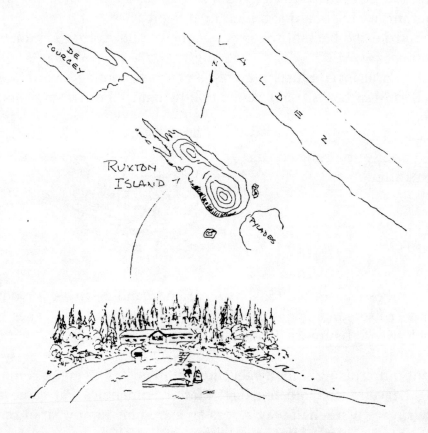

We spent more holiday time at Ruxton Island than anywhere else. Bill and Margaret Nayler bought it (and Pylades and several nearby smaller islands) for a few thousand dollars back in the dirty thirties when just about everything in the Gulf Islands was sold for back taxes.

We met Bill and Margaret early in our boating life. They were great friends of the legendary M. G. Hill of Yellow Point Lodge, just across the water, where Pat Tryon was a frequent guest. Early on we helped Bill and MG establish floating oyster beds on De Courcey and Ruxton islands and forever after reaped succulent rewards. The oysters grew on wires suspended from floating wooden rafts.

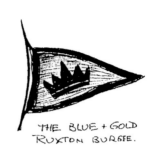

THE BLUE + GOLD
RUXTON BURGEE.

Amongst other things I will always remember Ruxton as the place where I kicked a 25-year smoking habit when a fierce bout of summer 'flu damn near reduced my breath rate to zero. Enid noticed I was a bit edgy for a couple of months but there weren't any more serious withdrawal symptoms. It was a mental battle, mostly, in my case, and a tough one. I playfully tried to substitute alcohol for tobacco at first but that wasn't much of an idea. Jeez, some days you just can't win.

But there were more significant memories of Ruxton that Enid and I will never forget. Like the Christmas morning we sat in the warm sunshine on the wharf drinking champagne cocktails with Bill and Margaret while the turkey slowly roasted to perfection ashore. It was such balmy summer-like weather that I pushed hard for a turkey roast on the sandy beach.

Overruled (as usual) by the distaff side. Later, under the moon and stars, utter calm prevailed as we savored liquors while carols dominated the airwaves.

There was something heavenly blissful about walking those Ruxton Island trails, so lovingly blazed by Bill and Margaret for beauty and contentment. There was an intense quiet — peace really — of being in friendly woods with nothing more ferocious than a deer or raccoon. The zesty sea air, mixed with the tang of the pines and other evergreens, blended into a heady perfume. At night in the soft glow of an oil lantern the atmosphere of blissful serenity was complete. We treasured those emotions, knowing they would not survive much longer. Every day pressure was growing to open such private paradises "to the public" which would paradoxically destroy their most precious asset — solitude.

Although Gulf Islanders value their privacy they are gregarious and socialize strenuously. One of Bill's favorite stories concerned four cronies who lived on Galiano Island right by Active Pass. One of them told his wife he "felt sick" and thought some ale might be the proper medicine. He picked up three of his buddies and rowed across the narrow but turbulent waterway to the pub on Mayne Island.

On the return trip in the pitch-black night the oarsman hit such a large semi-submerged log that he thought he had struck the beach and shouted, "Here we are — everybody out." And out they all jumped, right into the middle of the pass.

When our hero got home, soaking wet, his wife asked diplomatically if he was "still sick."

"Hell no," he replied, "I'm still drunk."

Of course my wife Enid (ex-First Mate) was quite right insisting I return to a permanent life ashore after our two unique years up the coast with the fisheries department. I was much more suited to life in the business world, and not unhappy to resume a career which eventually led me into the senior echelons of advertising and public relations — although it cost me my beloved PUTZY.

Today, 36 years later, I can still picture her as she lay forlornly at the sales dock at the VanIsle marina in Sidney. Geoff Simpson the yacht broker eventually sent a cheque to me in Ottawa but it could never cover the pain of parting from a dreamboat full of such precious memories.

Port-Red-Left   Toot-Toot !!

There was this keen young First Mate, you see, being examined for his master mariner's certificate by a crusty old deep-sea Captain. He had successfully answered many impossible questions and was silently praying for a quick end to the ordeal.

"Aye, you've done well so far," said the ferocious Captain, "but I have one last problem for ye to solve."

"Yes Sir."

"The situation is this: Y'er anchored in an exposed harbor with a fifteen knot onshore breeze blowing. After an hour the wind picks up to 20 knots and there's promise of more to come. What do ye do, eh?"

"I put out a second anchor, Sir."

"Aye. And after another hour the wind is up to 30 knots. What now?"

"Put out another anchor, Sir."

"And when the wind reaches 40 knots?"

"Another anchor, Sir."

"And 50 knots?"

"Another anchor, Sir."

"Hold fast there a minute! Jest where in hell are ye getting all those goddamn anchors?"

"From the same place, Sir, that you're getting all that goddamn wind."

Captain Scott Steen of the 136-foot yacht MARIJEAN of Vancouver laughed uproariously at his own joke and threatened me even worse treatment when it came time for my own Master's examination. Sadly this was not to be for I was serious about establishing a new life ashore after two glorious years aboard PUTZY on fisheries patrol. But that didn't preclude the occasional "holiday" as First Mate on the MARIJEAN.

I took a liking to Captain Steen the first moment I clapped eyes on him, and as events turned out he was of a similar mind.

This happened in Mazatlan where my wife and I were spending the winter. A Mexican doctor suggested I visit the hospital and "cheer up" a wounded compatriot.

Not that he needed sympathy, for his injured elbow had healed well, but he was desperate to swap news and gossip in English with another sailor, which we did at some length over icy rum swizzles amid the cool tropical shrubbery and brilliant flowers that decorated the out-patients courtyard.

Scott was a hefty six-foot-two master mariner with twinkley eyes and a ready smile. He could spin a good yarn and appreciated a willing listener and we soon became the best of friends. When his ship returned from a cruise to the Galapagos under a substitute captain and the owner, H. R. MacMillan the lumber baron had flown home to Vancouver, Scott welcomed us aboard to celebrate his recovery.

There is absolutely *nothing* that makes you feel more like *someone* than to be met at the town quay by a uniformed sailor and ferried out in a smart runabout to a luxury yacht anchored mid-harbor in a tropical port. And there, under the stars on a broad after-deck trimmed with soft, colored lights, to be served drinks and a fine dinner by a white-clad staff as the honored guests of a genial host.

Scott, the bachelor, was making great progress that evening with his lady-love Carmen, a bouncy Mexican divorcee, until a crewman appeared, quite tipsy, in a dress, makeup, wig and high heels. At this the cook turned sulky and started to pout and the chief engineer laughed so hard he fell off his chair and the evening ended somewhat chaotically.

The MARIJEAN (named after the owner's two daughters) spent several months each winter at Mazatlan holidaying, deep-sea fishing and running scientific cruises for the Vancouver Aquarium to the Galapagos Islands, South America, the West Indies and Hawaii.

During the rest of the year, based in Vancouver, the MARIJEAN continued her philanthropic work and rescued many abandoned Indian totems and artifacts from the Queen Charlotte Islands and other northern coastal sites which were restored and donated to museums.

At other times the owner kept MARIJEAN busy visiting his coastal forestry and fishing operations and running an enjoyable schedule of business/fishing trips which I have observed command a high priority in the affairs of millionaires.

It was for just this latter sort of trip that Scott first signed me on as First Mate. We were bound for Bag Harbor in the Queen Charlotte Islands where the owner and friends would fly in to fish for coho.

Moments after I reported aboard the experienced crew (one engineer, cook and steward all doubled as deckhands) cast off and we were under way. Scott was on the bridge and one engineer was on duty below manning the brass telegraphs.

"Nothing to it," said Scott with a satisfied grin as we headed out of the harbor. "She's all yours. Set a course for Seymour Narrows. I'm going below for breakfast."

Alone in the wheelhouse as we passed under the Lions Gate Bridge, I found myself humming " . . . what a capital ship for an ocean trip is the galloping MARIJEAN . . . " I was that excited. And proud, too, of the responsibility of running my first large, deep-sea yacht.

The MARIJEAN (like movie actor John Wayne's WILD GOOSE and Victoria entrepreneur Bob Wright's MARABELLE) had been built of wood for WW2 duty in the U.S. Navy as a minesweeper. Mr. MacMillan bought the 135-foot vessel at a war-surplus sale for a reputed $8,000 and then spent a bundle converting her for personal use. Four single outside cabins on the main deck and two double cabins below deliberately limited accommodation to select friends. An intimate mahogany-paneled dining saloon was well appointed with quality silver, linen, china and stemware. Adjoining it was a spacious lounge which led out to the large open after deck.

The crew (including me) had our pick of quarters in the large foc'sle which contained toilets, showers and laundry laid on for the original Navy crew of 60. The bridge deck was Scott's domain. He enjoyed a comfortable cabin/office just abaft the large wheelhouse and chartroom. Two 24-foot tenders hung in davits nearby.

Below, in the huge engine room, sat the main propulsion — two 500 hp diesels — and the auxiliary motors and machinery to provide electricity, forced air ventilation and hot water for taps and heating. Just ahead (and connected to the galley above) were large storage lockers and a walk-in deepfreeze full of fish, meat, poultry and pastry. A thoughtfully-stocked wine cellar lay nearby.

Commands from the bridge were sent to the engine room by traditional polished-brass telegraphs which meant that an engineer had to stand by the signal at all times when underway. The first time I rang down a signal there was a long pause before the response and I mentioned this to Scott.

THE CAPTAIN

"Have a heart," he said, "this isn't the Navy.

"There's only one engineer on duty at a time and he has a lot of other things to do when we're under way. It helps to warn him on the phone or voice-pipe before ringing down signals."

Normal procedure on a small vessel during our week-long trips to the Queen Charlotte Islands or around the west coast of Vancouver Island would be for the Captain and the Mate to share watches on the bridge. But Scott was such a chatty, agreeable type that he seldom went below and I was very much the same.

We had good fun together (while the automatic pilot did the work) seeing who could plot the better course and track it more accurately with radar and depth sounder. Or compute speed and position by bearings, landmarks or loran. Or work out accurate arrival times in areas prone to confusing tidal currents.

After dark on a clear night Scott was in his element shooting three-star fixes with his sextant. I tried to play down this technical virtuosity by pointing out that most nights we were securely at anchor in a known position, but the fact was that I knew very little about stars and nothing at all about sextants.

There were other things I didn't know about, too, like that bloody anchor winch. I was used to the simple electric winches found on pleasure boats and was quite awed by the MARIJEAN's six-foot high hydraulic monster with multiple levers and wheels.

Finally, under shouted commands from an impatient skipper in the wheelhouse, I got the chain running out.

"One shot will be enough," Scott shouted.

"What the hell is one shot?" I shouted back.

"Ninety feet."

So that's 15 fathoms, I muttered to myself, and this chain is flagged every 10 fathoms. Jesus, there must be an easier way.

"Looks OK right there," Scott shouted.

"Aye, Captain," I replied thankfully and locked down the dogs on the gypsy. At least we had avoided talking about cables -- a unit of 600 feet or one-tenth of a nautical mile.

Scott had a healthy appetite and liked the cook to serve up large hot meals three times a day for the crew. One day, bound for Barkley Sound on the west coast of Vancouver Island, lunch time arrived just as we began to feel the full force of the open Pacific swell which a stiff westerly had topped with a rollicking chop.

As the motion increased, things started banging around below and I needed a firm grip on the overhead grab rail to keep from lurching around the wheelhouse.

The skipper looked at his watch and sent me below for lunch, where I joined a subdued crew. As the cook dished up soup, he asked if anyone wanted the bowl nailed down. The second engineer gave him a glassy stare and headed rapidly for the lee rail. The steward got through the soup but when the roast beef arrived he too left. That left the cook and me, and he didn't look so hot either.

"Sure glad to have you aboard," said Scott when I relieved him for lunch. The crew all bloody seasick we're only five miles offshore."

One morning, tied up at the wharf at Ucluelet, we woke to a thick fog. Time was pressing and Scott soon had our departure from the narrow, twisting harbor neatly figured out.

He laid out several short compass headings on the chart, and measured them for time . . . two minutes here, one there, five to avoid the small island, and so forth. The maneuver was too delicate for the automatic pilot so I stood by to swing the large spoked wheel by hand onto the compass courses while Scott watched the radar screen and barked out commands. As we got under way, Scott nipped back and forth between the chart table, the compass, the radar and the fathometer which was blipping out the depth of water under our keel. If one of the three instruments didn't jibe with our estimated position there would be an anxious moment running a check all around.

As we were clearing the harbor, Scott asked me to double-check the radar. Half a mile ahead a strong blip indicated a motionless vessel. We could hear no whistle, or answer to our own.

When the blip was within a hundred yards we stopped the engines and put the wheel over. Slowly we drifted into a cave-like clearing in the fog and scared up several hundred seagulls floating placidly on the oily swells.

Scott and I were talking one day about navigation and I mentioned how a metal ashtray near the compass on PUTZY had caused so much deviation (30 degrees!) that I had almost gone on the Sand Heads near Vancouver.

"Pal of mine wasn't so lucky," said Scott. "He was running a fish packer which is almost all night work, as you know, and lonely.

"Anyway this particular dark and stormy night he was sitting in the wheelhouse drinking coffee to stay awake and wondered why it was taking such a long time to close the Fraser River lightship.

"Finally he went out on the after deck for a breath of air and looking over the side realized that although the engine was running full blast there was no wake out astern. His compass course had been a bit off and he'd been aground on those damn Sand Head for who knows how long!"

Same kind of thing happened to Columbus, I said.

"Oh? How's that?"

"Well, originally he set out to discover America with four ships."

"History says there were only three. "

"No, there were four at the beginning. One had compass error and sailed over the edge."

I was happy to find, in the MARIJEAN wheelhouse, two small signs on a beam near the whistle (horn) control handle. Just like I had aboard PUTZY. These little signs always remind me of the story about an old Admiral who was being praised at his retirement party for the brilliant way he had directed his ships in sea battles.

"But I noticed , Sir, that when your fleet was in action you continually referred to a small black notebook. Would that perchance contain some precious words of wisdom for future engagements?"

"Harrumph," snorted the old sea dog loudly, "yes, yes . . . you might say that. I carried a little notebook book next to my heart ever since I was a midshipman. It contains only seven words, but words that are vital to successful maneuvers at sea."

The silence was palpable as the questioner continued, "and pray what might those words of wisdom be, Sir?"

"A rule a sailor must never forget."

"Yes?"

"Turning starboard, one blast. Port, two blasts."

The first couple of evenings at anchor I noticed the crew helping themselves to beer from the ship's stores and marveled at their nerve in swiping it so openly. When I finally learned it was their own private stock, supplied by the owner, I insisted on double rations to catch up.

Scott and I ate with the rest of the crew at a large table in a corner of the galley. If there were guests aboard, unused wine from the dining saloon found its way to our table. Even when we were alone the steward produced bottles he had stored away earlier which made for convivial dining.

Mr. MacMillan was quite particular about the wines he served guests and we had a fine cellar aboard. If he wasn't aboard to preside at dinner, he would instruct Scott to limit the liquor and wines served to guests. Fortunately he was not so strict with the crew so long as we humored the guests and caused no trouble.

I often felt like a fifth wheel as the crew swung into well-practised routines for shipboard tasks. But all such efficiency was eclipsed when we tied up to disembark guests. Zip, the lines were ashore. Zip, up came the baggage. Zip, out went the gangplank. Zip, the guests were on their way in pre-ordered taxis. We panted with the effort but we also sighed with relief. The MARIJEAN was ours again.

"Steward," the Captain would say, "break out the rum in my cabin and let all hands splice the main brace," the traditional sailors' reward for a job well done.

DOOR TO THE CAPTAIN'S CABIN

The yacht herself felt the release of tensions and seemed to romp homewards with a friskiness she had not dared to indulge while strange feet tramped her decks. Tongues were loosened about the peculiarities of our guests and the cook once became so excited describing how a female guest had scorned his clam chowder because it was Friday and he had spiced it with ham, that he ate his dessert before his soup.

The Captain kept his observations to himself, although I remember his heavy hand on the ear-shattering horn when obnoxious guests appeared on the foredeck in the fog after partying all night.

More than anything, on those runs home, I looked forward to a bath. Showers we had in abundance on the MARIJEAN but for all her luxury she lacked a good, old-fashioned tub.

Besides, at sea with Scott I was only the First Mate while at home I was The Captain, albeit shore bound.

⚓   ⚓   ⚓

Captains Orders

In pleasure-boating circles, wives are commonly referred to as "The First Mate," a subordinate rank which can easily give an unwary spouse ("The Captain") a totally false sense of superiority. Let's not forget that even Noah had his wife by his side when he sailed off in the Ark.

With such precedents in mind, I was quick to pay heed when my wife Enid made a casual observation while I was writing these pages about boating.

"Surely a memoir about our adventures at sea would be incomplete without mention of our honeymoon," she said.

I was tempted to remind her that on that occasion we were not holidaying on our small family cruiser but crossing the North Atlantic on an ocean liner, when better sense (for once) prevailed.

"Indeed so," I lied smoothly, "I'm working on an item about remarkable ocean liners at this very moment."

Enid first came to Canada, from England, on the Cunard ship Aquitania as a guest of the department of veterans affairs. She was the widow of an RCAF pilot and was attached to a party of war brides which Canadian servicemen had left behind when they were repatriated at the end of hostilities. The Chief Engineer took a special interest in her unusual situation and went out of his way to make her voyage a pleasant experience.

A year later Enid and I were married and decided to return to London where Enid's cosy flat in Paddington lay waiting. As luck would have it we travelled on the Aquitania but it was a strange crossing. Although it was almost two years after the end of the war, the Aquitania still operated as a troopship. For that role, the fine furnishings of this luxury liner had been replaced by utility chairs, tables, cutlery and china. Married couples, like us, were separated and slept in large single-sex wards although we were together all the rest of the time. Enid's friend, the Chief Engineer, was still aboard and offered us all the comforts of his spacious suite to ease the otherwise restrictive conditions under which we were travelling. An unusual honeymoon, to be sure, but one easy to remember, for it ill-behooves a bridegroom to ever forget such a time and place.

The Aquitania, pre-war, was considered the most beautiful ship in the world. She was the best and most opulent of a trio of floating palaces which Cunard built early in the century as Britain sought to wrest control of the lucrative North Atlantic passenger trade from Germany. To emphasize prestige and luxury, the three liners were built larger than those of the German rivals and each carried four huge funnels.

The Mauretania was first in service, followed by The Lusitania which was sunk within sight of Ireland, with a loss of 1200, by a German submarine at the beginning of World War One. The Aquitania was launched in 1913 at John Brown's shipyard on the Clyde in Scotland. During WW1 she was dazzle-painted and served as a hospital ship. But as soon as hostilities ended, she was re-fitted and modestly described as the most costly and lavishly decorated ship afloat.

Competition on the North Atlantic after WW1 was intense. The German ships Bremen and Europa were supreme, each winning the coveted Blue Ribbon for speed and excellence.

The theory of marine interior decor in those days was to make the wealthy passengers forget they were on the rambunctious Atlantic and merely spending a few restful days at their favorite luxury hotel on dry land. Thus Bremen was a cathedral of steel, the Italian liner Rex was all Roman grandeur and Latin bravura with an interior like a palazzo. The French liner Normandie was like an old chateau -- an odor of tobacco, oil and cognac seemed embedded in the hand-carved woods in the library.

The Germans first created this image, using a British design team which had perfected such hotels as the Ritz in London, and British shipbuilders were quick to polish it. The Germans were first to develop a bulbous bow which pushed through the water more quickly and with less fuss than the regular knife-edge bow. The British were first to weld hull plates instead of using rivets, making a smooth hull that would slip more economically through the water. Both countries developed oil-fired boilers to generate steam for the engines, doing away with up to 350 sweaty coal-shoveling stokers per vessel -- surely one of the dirtiest jobs in maritime history.

Aquitania's two-inch thick Sheffield steel double bottom provided a sturdy platform for lavish marble decor and statuary, elaborate hand-carved woodwork, ornamental staircases and glass-enclosed promenade decks. She was the first Cunard liner to offer a swimming pool and electric elevators. Money was lavished on ornate public lounges, dining saloons, and distinctive suites and cabins. The most famous chef in the world, Cesar Ritz, planned the menus and over-saw every detail of the catering. This huge outlay of money (partly subsidized by the British government with the excuse that the ships could be converted into armed frigates in the event of war) enabled Cunard to win back the Blue Ribbon of the Atlantic as owners of the best, the fastest, the most prestigious passenger liners afloat.

Ocean ships had now become huge glorious hotels... ships of state... as nations competed for the North Atlantic trade. Public rooms, staterooms, suites, dining saloons (coffee and brandy was served in smaller salons) , writing rooms, library, smoking rooms were fitted out with fine tables and furniture, linens, crystal and cutlery and hand-carved exotic wood paneling and fine artwork to make a rich showcase of Edwardian elegance in the tradition of the English Manor House. At dinner, the company of 700 first-class passengers in formal clothes, gowns and jewels made a glittering sight.

The success of these magnificent ships laid a profitable basis for the development of the mighty Cunard super liners Queen Mary and Queen Elizabeth which were to prove so crucial to the Allied victory in World War Two.

Lunch à la Carte

SS Europa   Wednesday July 13, 1932

Hors d'Oeuvre:

Salad Opéra   Tomato Neptun
Eggs Andalouse   Canapé Alberta
Truffles of Goose Liver   Rissoles Lucy
Cassolettes Mascotte   Fillet of Smoked Mackerel
Bonne Bouchée   Herring Suédoise
Royans Vatel   Aspic de Volaille Rachel
Sprats in Tomato Sauce   Cornichons
Stuffed Olives   Royal Pickles
Rouget Oriental   Artichoke Hearts in Oil   Scallions

Cold Dishes:

Fresh Hard Shell Crabs Argenteuil   Leg of Lamb with Mint Jelly
Poularde Yorkshire Style   Roast Loin of Veal Fontainebleau
Duckling with Fruit Salad   Prime Ribs of Beef Denise
Brunswick Pâté of Liver, Sauce Gloucester   Smoked Westphalian Ham
Boiled Prague Ham   Choice of Sausage

Soups:

Puree Georgette   Iced Consommé Double   Chervil Cream Soup with Butter Dumplings
Chicken Broth in Cup

Eggs:

Omelet Rouennaise   Poached Eggs Benedict

Fish:

Fried Fillet of Shad, Chicago Salad   Escalope of Halibut Helgoland

Entrées:

Larded Cushion of Veal Concorde   Boiled Turkey Virginia
Esterhazy Rostbraten   Cromesquis Bergère

From the Grill (10-15 Minutes):

English Mutton Chop, Saratoga Chips   Guinea Chicken with Currant Jelly
Pig's Kidney Ludwig XV.

Salads:

Lettuce   Beet-Root   Romaine   Mixed   Martini
Dressings: St. Rudolph   Chiffonade   Cream   French

New vegetables:

Spinach American   Creamed Parsnips
Green Peas   Tomato au Four
Buttered Sliced Beans   Stuffed Small Cabbage Heads
Corn on Cob with Butter   Purée Suzette
Kobirabi Bourgeoise   Sauted Chanterelles

Vegetables:

Lentils German Style   Greencorn Fritters   Steamed Rice

Potatoes:

Baked Idaho   Baked Sweet   Boiled New   Vauban
Strasburg   Croquettes   Bartholdi   Copeaux

Sweets and Compote:

Gooseberry Tart with Baiser   Berlin Doughnuts   Cold Danish Pudding, Vanilla Sauce
Crème Montholon   Mixed Compote   Compote of Fresh Fruit   Compote of Cherries

Ice Cream:

French Vanilla Ice Cream   Coupe Stella   Neapolitan Ice Cream, Wafers

Cheese:

Dutch   Primula   Port Salut   Roquefort   Camembert Brie   Philadelphia
Pumpernickel   Radishes   Soda Crackera
Fruit In Season
Demi Tasse   Sanka Demi-Tasse   Tea

Dinner

S.S. Europa Wednesday, July 13th, 1932

Hors d'Oeuvre:
    Malossol Caviare   Iced Musk Melon   Table Celery

Soups:
    Velouté   Vénitienne   Chicken Broth Brunoise   Consommé Double à Ia Moelle en Tasse
        Mille-fanti

Fish:
    Poached Rhine Salmon, Sauce Choron   Fillet of Pike Épicurienne, Cucumber Salad
    Little Neck Clam Fritters with Ketchup

Special Dish To-Day:
    Cumberland Ham in Burgundy Porte Maillot

Entrées:
    Saddle of Venison Romanoff   Filet Mignon, Green Peas, Parisian Potatoes
    Supréme of Squab Bodiska   Lobster Thermidor

Cold Dishes:
    Tenderloin Steak Garnished   Suprême of Quail Impromptu

Roasts:
    Saddle of Spring Lamb, Mint Sauce   Stuffed Pomeranian Gosling   Chalons Chicken en Casserole

From the Grill (10-15 Minutes):
    Sirloin Steak, Montpellier Butter   Veal Cutlet Fleury   Capon Liver with Bacon en Brochette

Salads:
    Lettuce   Escarole   Endives   Iceberg   Ninon
    Dressings: Special, French, Ladard, Club

New Vegetables:
    Cauliflower Polonaise Haricots Verts Maitre d'Hôtel Sauted Cucumbers Celery Rebecca
    Stuffed Tomato   Parisian Carrots   Braised Shallots   Purée Freneuse

Vegetables:
    Gnocchl Romain   Macaroni Italienne   Glazed Chestnuts   Steamed Rice

Potatoes:
    Baked Sweet   Baked Idaho   Boiled New   Julienne Nostitz   Petits Fours   Lyonnaise
    Carême   Biarritz

Sweets and Compote:
    Soufflé Marquise   Charlotte Metternich   Mixed Compote   Crêpes Parisienne
    Compote of Californian Peaches Marrons Pièmontaise Compote of Fresh Fruit

Ice Cream
    French Vanilla Ice Cream   Biscuit Tortoni Ice Cream, Palais des Dames
    Strawberries Renaissance

Assorted Cheese

Fruit in Season   Nuts   Raisins   Figs

Demi-Tasse   Sanka Demi-Tasse

When I was a young lad there was no other way to cross the oceans of the world than by ship. The trip to Europe took at least a week, often longer, and so strong was the romance and tradition of the sea that exhilarating memories lingered a lifetime.

As they did for my father, and my grandfather -- indeed, in only slightly different degrees of time and comfort, back four centuries to the voyages of Columbus.

I was a six-year-old schoolboy in Montreal when my grandfather died in Hastings, England. My father booked our family of four on a CPR liner for a two-month visit to his homeland. I remember the intense thrill of the evening when my young sister Monica and I sneaked away to crews quarters where a mouth-organ band of sailors enthralled us with salty, foot-stomping shanties.

Of course our parents were frantic to find us "missing" and we were soon returned to the family cabin where we excitedly told them that the mast of the ship was hollow and we had seen the hole in the bottom where sailors entered to climb up to the crow's nest. They were not much amused.

On our return to Montreal, the customs people enraged my father by making a huge fuss about my collection of fishermen's cork floats that I had picked up on the beaches around Hastings. They said a permit was required to import cork and only relented after my father heatedly protested that this was a ludicrous way to assess a small boy's holiday treasures.

By the time I made my two wartime crossings on the Queen Elizabeth, there was once again no indication of the pre-war elegance of the North Atlantic superships. The 10-year-old Queen Mary, on which Cunard was said to have spent £ 4 million, had been stripped of her finery and converted to a troopship.

The Queen Elizabeth, launched at the beginning of WW2, started life as an austere troopship. The two sister ships ferried millions of military personnel to Europe, and back, and contributed greatly to the Allied victory.

The details of my two wartime crossings aboard the Q.E. played a key role in my first volume of Memoirs, entitled "The Flying Game, (ISBN 1-55212-513-0 which is available through www.trafford.com).

At the end of the war, the Queen Elizabeth carried tens of thousands of Allied soldiers, sailors and airmen back to Canada, the United States and Australia. Finally, with a well-deserved sigh of relief, the world's largest troopship sailed home to the Clyde for a rest and a complete facelift.

Her cabins and saloons which had thronged with 20,000 troops each voyage were rebuilt into a luxurious oasis where 2200 peacetime passengers could be pampered by a crew of 1500. The original furnishings and fittings which had been ordered before the war were brought out of storage and magically transformed the drab troopship "Lizzie" into the ultimate symbol of elegance.

As such, the Queen Elizabeth reigned for 30 years, more than fulfilling the dreams of her owners, and was the envy of maritime nations the world over.

By 1973, however, the taste of world travelers had changed dramatically. Leisure and luxury were out, speed was in, and ocean liners were giving way to air liners.

And so, at the relatively young age of 33, the Queen Elizabeth found herself outdated and generations removed from the disco cruise ships which were beginning to develop a swinging holiday trade for the masses. The dowager Queen Elizabeth was sold for $2.3 million to a syndicate which proposed she continue life as a floating university. But as she was being converted in Hong Kong a vicious fire broke out, sending her to the bottom of the harbor on January 1,1972. Sabotage perhaps, but nothing was ever proven. Divers salvaged 45,000 tons of metal from her hull and the skeletal remains were towed out to sea and sunk.

⚓   ⚓   ⚓

Long-forgotten memories of building simple radios when I was a teenager, and later using advanced equipment during many years of flying and boating, were revived in 1999 by the official announcement that world-wide shipping would henceforth use satellite-based communications systems in place of Morse code radio telegraphy.

Samuel Morse devised his easy code of dots and dashes to represent letters and numbers, and the simple instrument to send and receive these electrical pulses over a wire, about 150 years ago. Newspapers, railroads, shipping and businesses around the world took quickly to this new communication system and soon tied the world together with overland wires and undersea cables.

Mariners were able to adopt Morse's code when the radio was invented and Morse's dots and dashes could be sent through the air. For almost 100 years the familiar SOS distress signal (Save Our Souls?) of three dots, three dashes, three dots was the universal way to call for help in an emergency, and the two letters CQ (dash dot, dash dot -- dash, dash, dot, dash) provided world-wide amateur radio enthusiasts ("hams") with a common calling card.

The sender of a Morse code signal can be easily located if he is in a fixed position on land, or hooked onto a telegraph wire. But the mariner at sea, in addition to sending out his SOS distress call, had to define the ships position, often just a guesstimate which he might not even have time to include in the distress message.

Today's modern global positioning system (GPS) relays radio signals through a group of satellites in space and automatically calculates the sender's position with great accuracy which makes for quick and effective rescue work. The GPS transmitter/receiver is a small computer with a display screen and selection of buttons for information input.

The old Morse code was one of the first things I had to master when I joined the RCAF in the summer of 1939. It was the main method of aerial communicating, by lights or radio, with other aircraft and the ground. The electrically-generated dots and dashes (short and long pulses) were produced by a small instrument like a typewriter key and received through earphones.

Morse code radio signals could span much greater distances than voice (microphone) signals and could themselves be coded to provide added secrecy. The radio transmitter could be easily tuned to different frequencies to further avoid eavesdroppers.

Morse code operators on ships reached their heyday during the Titanic sinking in 1912. They were called wireless officers then and for a long time were the only "officer" on the ship. (The others were the Captain, licensed as "Master", the First (second, third, or more) Mates, Bosun, Purser, Engineer, etc.)

A top-notch Morse code operator could read, and send, more than 40 words a minute. Each person had a distinctive touch as he pounded the key, which was called his "signature" and was easily recognized by others. Men who spent years sending Morse began "thinking" in Morse, and even dreamed of conversations with their fellow operators in dots and dashes.

Morse telegraphers were everywhere. One in each railway station kept the trains moving on time, and relayed messages up and down the line. Post offices and commercial telegraph centers sent telegrams quickly and efficiently around the world in Morse. Newspapers enjoyed special rates (I seem to remember paying a penny a word to send dispatches from Ottawa to the Toronto Telegram in those days) and no doubt other high-volume users like the financial markets.

Morse operators were often radio technicians as well, trained to keep their equipment in good repair and improvise a way around breakdowns. My long-time friend Ray Mackness was such a man and had a delightful fund of stories about the old days of Morse code telegraphy.

When Ray graduated from high school around 1930, prohibition was in full swing in the U.S. and his home town port was a major exporter of bootleg booze destined for thirsty Americans. Large cargo ships which could carry upwards of 50,000 cases of liquor, legally cleared customs in Vancouver, bound for exotic foreign ports around the world. For a variety of reasons (mostly "engine problems") many ships found themselves drifting 12 or 15 miles off the U.S. Pacific Coast, where small American speedboats came out to load up on the illegal booze and sneak it into safe US harbors. A lovely setup -- the parched Americans took all the risk in breaking their prohibition laws and avoiding armed coast guard patrols while the Canadian ships sat safely, and legally, outside the 12-mile boundary reaping huge profits.

But how did the American smugglers know when booze was nearby and how did they make their furtive rendezvous? By radio, and cryptic Morse code messages like "Mother will be in hospital until tomorrow" in which the word hospital stood for a pre-arranged position of the booze ship.

And who did all the radio work? Why special operators who were put on the ships by the "exporters" for these special trips.

Enter Ray Mackness, jobless high-school graduate, who answered an advertisement by a Vancouver secretarial school which guaranteed a job to graduates of their radio course. A golden opportunity to be gainfully employed in the depression years and Ray couldn't enroll quick enough.

"I thought at the time it was rather strange for would-be radio announcers to be spending so much time in school on radio construction and repair, and learning Morse code," he said later, "but remember, those were the dirty thirties and jobs were damn hard to come by."

And so Ray went to sea, exchanging cryptic messages with shadowy American characters until the U.S. finally admitted that prohibition was definitely not working and called off their 14-year "noble experiment" (said President Herbert Hoover) in 1933. By this time Ray had built up a background of practical radio experience and was able to land a job with the CBC in Vancouver where, apart from overseas service in WW2, he remained as an announcer until his untimely death in the 1960s, an unsung hero of Canada's immensely profitable rum-running trade.

Retirement Cruising
in MARTEN

Thirteen years after I sold my dreamboat PUTZY and moved to the east to advance the family fortunes I found myself back on Vancouver Island, casually *(ho-ho)* visiting yacht brokerages to see what was on the market. And on a frosty February afternoon I discovered what was to be the last and longest-enduring yacht to fly the Furniss flag.

My wife Enid, anxious to resume her old title as First Mate, and I had driven to Sidney to re-visit DUART, a rather spiffy 30-footer in gleaming mahogany with white vinyl upholstery, chrome ports and laid decks. And an owner in a tight cash bind pleading for offers around $25,000.

As we walked along the float to the boathouse our affable yacht broker urged us to cast an eye over MARTEN which had come on the market about five minutes earlier and was conveniently berthed next door.

Love at first sight. MAR-
TEN was one of six 28-foot
lap-strake express cruisers designed by Thornton Grenfell of
Vancouver and built in the local Clark Brothers yard for the
B.C. fisheries department. She
had recently been overhauled
and re-engined with a monstrous (550 cubic-inch) Ford
marine gas engine.

She was dry and sweet-smelling thanks to sound construction, thor-
ough upkeep, oil stove heating and boathouse protection. I couldn't get
my checkbook out quick enough. $17,500.

On the water MARTEN ran smoothly and quietly although the electric
fuel pump clicked away at a frightening pace. But what the hell ... marine
gas was only 86 cents a gallon and we could loaf along quite economically
at 8 knots, just below planing speed, while holding the top speed of 14
knots (and 7 gallons per hour) in reserve for emergencies. We had tank-
age for 110 gallons which gave us a cruising range of around 220 miles.

A week later we arrived aboard in a snowstorm with supplies for the
christening party. The oil stove soon had MARTEN cozy and warm and
our guests voted to stay in the boathouse and enjoy hearty rounds of
rosé champagne, wine and cheese. My stockbroker, a bearded Royal
Navy veteran of WW2, confidently predicted we'd soon pick up enough
loose change in the market to pay for this new toy.

And so we began what turned out to be 12 years of most pleasurable
cruising aboard MARTEN. Being retired, time was no object and two trips
lasted six months each. Adding in the hundreds of shorter ones the log
book shows we lived aboard an astounding total of 997 days -- more than
two and a half years!

But it was relaxed cruising and we spent a lot of time leisurely explor-
ing remote bays and beaches and revisiting the scenes of our fishery patrol years aboard PUTZY. During our dozen golden years in MARTEN
we travelled 16,400 nautical miles compared to the 34,700 we had covered during six years in PUTZY.

It was some months after we bought MARTEN that we spent more than a single night aboard. I had formally declared myself retired the year before, grown a wild bushy beard and enrolled in the Victoria School of Art. I had been drawing and painting for years and wanted to develop this hobby.

But while art school was stimulating, it was also damn hard work. Nine to five, five or more days a week, and homework, for God's sake, at the ballpark drawing people.

"I don't think you're temperamentally suited to the classroom environment," one of the instructors said sympathetically when I dropped out after the first year. That was true, but the lack of time to enjoy MARTEN was what really bugged me. Surely a mature 60-year-old could study art and go boating at the same time, and so I did.

Over the years MARTEN helped us re-explore the Gulf Islands, Desolation Sound, Johnstone Strait and the unspoiled havens around Kingcome Inlet and Simoon Sound. But boating had become a more popular recreation since our days in PUTZY and we found we had to start earlier and cruise farther north each year to find the peace and solitude of old.

Fred and Emma Wastell were still living at Telegraph Cove, growing old like the rest of us, with boundless equanimity. My old friend Harry, the fisheries inspector at Alert Bay, had moved to Victoria but I learned that modern fishery patrol officers earned four times as much as in my day.

My Cousin Spike (the Vietnam war fighter pilot I wrote about in "Memoirs One — The Flying Game," (www.trafford.com ISBN 1-55212-513-0) had built a new house on Berry Island and we spent happy hours fishing and flying around the coast in his Cessna floatplane.

Minstrel Island, our lively headquarters during the second year of PUTZY's fishery patrol days, had gone to pot. The large store where we had bought hardware, clothing, meat and groceries had burned down and never been replaced.

No fuel was available at the wharf. The beer parlor was still there, in the hotel, and a couple of fishermen were loading bottles of brew aboard a gillnetter at 10 o'clock in the morning -- one familiar sight!

Through the Blow Hole we found a new gas dock in Lagoon Cove and a marina filled with sports fishermen who had discovered the joys of Knight Inlet just around the point.

Alert Bay had changed little. Four pubs, liquor store and a special "Indian Club" in the basement of the old school were doing a roaring business. The wharf where PUTZY had once drawn gunfire had been re-located near the new ferry to Port NcNeill. Seven radio-controlled cabs (5 in the old days) raced around the seven miles of road.

Change was everywhere in our old fishery patrol area. The remains of a large wharf on one beach prompted the Mate to remark that this whole coast had become an area of "remains" -- abandoned houses, farms, derelict boats, disused canneries, disintegrating wharves, abandoned logging vehicles and machinery -- a sad monument to a once-prosperous scene.

The old days may not have been "better" but they were certainly more leisurely and amiable, and afforded inhabitants time to get to know and help each other to enjoy the bounty and beauty of the land.

We stopped one day for fuel at Kelsey Bay which hadn't changed much since our last visit 18 years earlier. The same decrepit gas dock, 30 feet in the air, where the hose was lowered down to boats scraping against the sticky, creosoted piles.

We summoned the attendant by telephone from his nearby house. When he eventually arrived he explained that it was his custom to take a glass or two of Rye whisky around four o'clock of an afternoon in the shade on his front porch. No one (least of all us) could complain about this civilized habit although it did seem odd that it was then only eleven o'clock in the forenoon.

After lunch the locals assured us that the weather outside the harbor had abated and we set out for Port Neville, seven miles up and across Johnstone Strait.

We quickly discovered that "abated" gave a false impression of the local weather and that Johnstone Strait was still its mean, nasty self which took fiendish delight in pitching and rolling us through some frightful water before we reached shelter. MARTEN took it all admirably ("...a magnificent sea boat" is the traditional way every owner describes the yacht he currently owns) although she proved to be a wet one and the windshield wipers couldn't keep up as she plunged ahead and flung spray ever higher and thicker until it became sheets of green water flowing down the decks. Several times the bow disappeared completely ("... say, that's never happened before" every owner asserts) and gallons poured into the foc'sle through the un-dogged hatch to drench our bunks and storage lockers thoroughly and repeatedly.

The Mate spent part of this miserable one-hour crossing below, holding down items that threatened to go into orbit, and part of the time in the cockpit in her floater jacket and a "let's abandon ship" look creasing her normally happy face. The crab net crashed down from its perch atop the wheelhouse and crockery and glass smashed around a bit, but give up the ship? **Never!**

And soon we were anchored in a flat calm in the inlet off Robber's Nob drying things out in the warm sunshine and calming frayed nerves with bracers of medicinal brandy.

We met many old friends on these travels, like John and Marna Noble who years ago owned the splendid old character yacht LADY ROYAL. She was a 25-ton Brixton trawler sailed to Canada in 1932 by "Brother Twelve," a weird little man with a small spiky beard and hypnotic eyes who established a mystic religious sect on DeCourcey Island.

As vigilantes from Nanaimo moved in to destroy his island paradise (and harem of wealthy devotees) Brother Twelve scuttled the LADY ROYAL in what is now Pirate's Cove marine park and fled to Europe with his lady love, leaving behind a huge buried treasure which to this day has never been found.

John' father, who lived on Quadra Island, salvaged the vessel and gave it to his son. John and his dynamic bride Marna lived aboard the LADY ROYAL for years, fishing for tuna off California and South America and chartering in the West Indies and the Pacific Northwest.

We also made many new friends, among which were two madcap engineers (one electrical and one aeronautical) who spent an hilarious evening designing a new system to combat MARTEN's chronic electrolysis. These worthies were unimpressed by MARTEN's little black box control and advocated new bonding wires everywhere to produce an "earth isolated" electrical system. They gave me pages of instructions and diagrams but it was all 'way over my head.

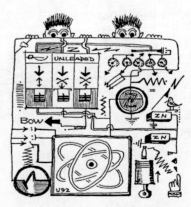

ELECTROLYSIS? NO PROBLEM ~~

The Mate and I spent a lot of time by ourselves in secluded anchorages reading, writing, drawing, painting, fishing, claming, oystering and just generally lazing about. From the outset we landed many fish in MAR-TEN. Some surprising catches by Enid, ever lucky, included:

A 30-pound ling cod

A 40-inch-long dogfish

Two fat coho plucked from the middle of a herring ball (When attacked by fish from below and gulls from above, schools of thousands upon thousands of silvery herring form a huge "ball" just below the surface)

A small but tasty rock cod which gillnetted itself trying to get at the bait in the crab net

A seagull which got one wing entangled in a trolling line when it made an ill-timed attack on a surface lure

Twenty-seven delectable Dungeness crabs, of which 26 were thrown back because they were females -- one day after the regulations had changed making females legal.

We often had so many fish and clams and oysters and crabs aboard (as well as store-bought meat and poultry) that we had to go out of our way to share this bounty with others before it spoiled for lack of ice.

Of course there were times when we had nothing and the log book recorded, "opened up a can of corned beef -- a welcome change."

Wine was served aboard MARTEN only when a meal was unanimously declared to be **"Gourmet"** and it was absolutely astounding how many times during our 12 years of cruising aboard MARTEN that we achieved this high level of culinary excellence -- the Mate with her choice of oil or propane stove, and ovens, and your Captain with his trusty barbecue. Absolutely "gourmet" repasts ranged through barbecued salmon, roast chicken or beef, crab fricassee, fried chicken wings, sautéed sole and even our favorite once-a-week dinner treat, bacon and eggs!

Birthdays, of course, called for **"Super Gourmet"** treatment, perhaps a superbly grilled platter of pork chops from the Mate's new butcher friend in Alert Bay, served with a choice of sparkling wines. After many years of marriage I've learned that while you must never ask a women her age it's absolutely imperative to observe her birthdays with flair and punctuality.

Simoon Sound is one of those places where you keep repeating to yourself, out loud, "My God, how quiet it is."

The occasional plane passes overhead, a few birds twitter, a fish splashes gently and then there is nothing but stillness so intense you can hear it. A fly, winging by, sounds like a motorcycle.

Curious seals often convoyed us as we rowed ashore for our daily walk. On the beach a humming bird hovered nose-to-nose with the Mate who was bundled in a bright red floater jacket like an exotic flower. Sometimes we foraged for water, fruit from abandoned orchards or hiked to nearby settlements for garden produce.

Sometimes we went ashore just to escape the blistering heat of a shimmering sea but mostly we went ashore just to enjoy mother nature's bountiful charms. The playful mink scampering around the rocky shore at low tide dining on kelp and mussels, the loons echoing the hills with their haunting cry, bald eagles patrolling majestically, squawking seagulls dropping clamshells on the rocks to break open their lunch, and an endless chorus of sound in the woods as robins, chickadees, red wings and tree frogs celebrated life.

158

There were deer browsing on fresh grass, large blue herons on toothpick legs stepping daintily through shallow tidal pools, observed by hawks, deer and raccoons. And the inevitable bear droppings and cougar tracks around fresh water sources.

Serene anchorages abounded. At one a fine driftwood stag sat quietly (and permanently) by the trees near our stern line. Not far away an old blackened stump which looked like a bear (they *all* look like bears) suddenly stood up and ambled off. On those infrequent occasions the Mate postponed the daily visit ashore "until the weather cleared" and contented herself with rowing to the nearest kelp bed to catch tasty rock cod on her spinning rod.

14 October 1999

Dear Colin,

Thanks for your kind words about my old tugboat drawing. You may (subconsciously?) recognize it -- the OB-1 which was owned by Jens Swenson who ran Lund Marine, in Lund, for more than 40 years. You can just see where I originally drew in the name, then obliterated it when I thought of using the drawing commercially.

Enie and I visited Lund, ("Gateway to the picturesque cruising grounds of Desolation Sound") many times during our four decades of yachting. I remember getting Jens to make me up a copper pipe fitting so that I could shut off the automatic bilge exit to prevent water coming *in*. He didn't sell me a valve, but took me out to his shop, in the back, and picked a small piece of copper pipe out of a junk box of stuff. Threaded the ends on his lathe, bent this, sized that, and voila, just what I needed. Think he charged me about a dollar and a half !

On our first or second visit "north" on Marten, about 1980, I ran over a small deadhead running into Malaspina Inlet. Limped (what else!) back to Lund where Jens hauled the boat and installed my spare prop. Because of the tides, we had to spend the night there. A couple of hours before dark, Jens fired up the OB-I and took us out fishing around that small chain of islands that has since become a marine park. Other guests aboard were Lionel and Frances (?) Something of the WVYC sloop WHITESHELL. This entry in my logbook isn't too clear, as it was written shortly after Jens brought us home; no fish, but a very happy bunch of sailors, fully topped up on his seemingly endless supply of Scotch.

I drew the tug three or four years ago when we last visited Lund, by car. There's a nifty motel (Beach Gardens) just near Grief Point where we often go, when the mood (and bank account) coincide. I didn't ask if old Jens lived (or had lived) in the house near the OB. But there was no mistaking the tug, and its revival of wonderful memories. I started the drawing in pencil, on site. Finished it, in ink, at home later.

Love to Ruth,

Harry & Enid

Living aboard a boat for long periods calls for a continuous program of maintenance. Painting, cleaning, repairing and refurbishing is necessary to keep boat and engine comfortable and reliable. Work aboard MARTEN increased greatly when we gave up the boathouse (annual rent had reached $2500) and opted for permanent canvas covers for extended cruises.

As the years whizzed by we noticed a great change in boats and the people who spent weekends and holidays cruising coastal waters. Plastics and fiberglass reduced maintenance. Inexpensive VHF radios with dozens of channels provided clear communications. Small reliable radars and satellite navigation were new toys.

YACHT "RIGOR MORTIS" and DINGHY "LITTLE STIFF"

Typical of the changing times were the names of boats. Instead of MARY, MARTEN or CORSAIR we found COOKIE MONSTER, BUTTERSCOTCH RIPPLE, BEER CAN and an endless stream of HAPPY HOOKERS. And COSTA-PLENTI, a fine 36-footer owned (perhaps) by the chap who runs a campground on Vancouver Island called COSTA LOTTA. An all time favorite was a radio transmission from "Charlie-Lima-Oscar-Charlie-Kilo-Whiskey-Oscar-Romeo- - - - - - - -" which eventually turned out to be CLOCKWORK ROCKET SHIP

More pleasure boats afloat with more inexperienced skippers brought on more distress calls and MARTEN took part in several rescues, well aware of the salvage rules which might eventually apply. One blustery night I heard an unusual SOS -- a 22-foot runabout reported to the Vancouver Coast Guard that it was aground on a "coral reef" just up-stream from the Second Narrows bridge in Vancouver harbor. After a pause, the Coast Guard radio operator said, gently, "by any chance, Sir, would you be aground on the mud banks?" "No" came the positive, prompt reply. "Definitely a coral reef." At this the cutter MOORHEN was dispatched to the rescue and all participants wisely discontinued further radio communication.

Large ships had trouble too -- a B.C. ferry ran on a reef at the southern entrance to Active Pass -- as well as smaller vessels with certified masters. One tugboat skipper, during his morning radio report to head office, mentioned that he had been aground "for three or four minutes" during the night. Asked what excuse could be given to the insurance company for running aground, the skipper promptly replied "insufficient water."

After more than 40 years of pleasure boating, our days afloat ended in 1985 when we traded our Victoria condo for a house at Columbia Beach near Parksville and switched to a land-based retirement lifestyle. No regrets, looking back, that we finally forsook the sea as a recreational playground. We like to think that we enjoyed the golden years of boating before the waterways and harbors became choked with hordes of boorish newcomers who imagined the Canada Shipping Act had something to do with importing lettuce from California.

At home I can look out the window and admire a thunderstorm without worrying whether the anchor is dragging or my bunk is getting soaked. Ah, the weather in coastal B.C. We only have two choices, really; the sublime and absolutely bloody awful. Logbooks of the Furniss fleet record a discouraging number of cold, stormy, wet spells. I'm often inclined to think that Captain Vancouver, who discovered this coast, got it right when he named our most popular cruising ground "Desolation Sound."

The End

ISBN 155212820-2

9 781552 128206